TAI
CHI
CHUAN

TAI CHI CHUAN

the philosophy of yin and
yang and its application

by Douglas Lee

This book is dedicated to my daughter,
Annameika Renora Oy Hing Lee,
and to my father-in-law, James Sainsbury, whose
spirit of naturalness and simplicity exemplified
the inner heart of Tai Chi.

Fifteenth Printing 1985

Graphic Design by Nancy Hom Lem
ISBN No. 0-89750-044-x

OHARA [] PUBLICATIONS, INCORPORATED
BURBANK, CALIFORNIA

acknowledgements————

Many thanks to: Master Raymond Y.M. Chung for teaching me the Yang Style of Tai Chi Chuan as he knew it.

My uncle John Wong, a noted calligrapher and linguist, for his translations of the Chinese upon which this book is based.

My sister-in-law Margaret Lee for her clarification of many of the poetic and symbolic meanings in Chinese which gave me greater insight into the background of Tai Chi forms.

Dr. Ron Eliosoff and his wife Janice for their great confidence in me and for her helpful editing of my writing which inspired me to complete this book for publication.

Joan Baille for all the time and effort that she spent with me in the shooting of all the photographs exhibited in this book; her generosity and patience in the development and printing of all the photographs; and the understanding and openness with which she accepted this task.

All those students and teachers for firing those probing questions which forced my mind to inquire openly and deeply until the answers came.

about the author

I was born the seventh member of a family of eight in Victoria, the capital of British Columbia, Canada, on March 28, 1941. I entered the martial arts at age twenty-three at a time when I was disillusioned and disenchanted with life and living. Since then I have slowly come to discover myself and the meaning and significance of life and living. During the four years that I was directly with the Vancouver Tai Chi Chuan Association I assisted the instructor and was M.C. and commentator at all demonstrations and annual club anniversary banquets. Since then I have taught privately and I am still doing so. I also taught publicly for the Vancouver Free University for one and one-half years. I taught for a short time for WHATCOM University at Bellingham, Washington, a growth potential group, and could have continued to do so if I could have arranged it to fit my shifts at work. I am by trade an artificial kidney technician at the Vancouver General Hospital. I have been working there for over nine years.

preface

The summer evening of '65 was beautiful. The sky was clear blue. The air was warm in the sunlight and a comfortable cool in the shade. The weather was perfect for my evening stroll. As I was passing by a storefront on Jackson Street I peered through the windows. What I saw overwhelmed me. I was struck by the beauty of the movements. The movements were so soft, so light and so graceful. It was so charming that I knew I had to learn it. That was my beginning in the art of Tai Chi Chuan.

When I first joined the Vancouver Tai Chi Chuan Studio, Tai Chi Chuan, was almost an unknown art in this country. Tai Chi Chuan was a closely guarded art form normally reserved only for those of Chinese extraction. The club I joined, however, was open to all nationalities, every color and race. It was the first Chinese martial arts school in the Vancouver area to be so liberal.

At the time I joined, the English speaking students represented a small but sizeable minority. Within a few years they became the majority and comprise to this day over 85 percent of the members. In learning Tai Chi Chuan the English speaking majority had one major obstacle to hurdle: the instructor spoke very little, if any, English and all the guides to learning which were tacked to the walls were in Chinese. To help the English speaking majority, I began slowly over a period of time to translate all the instructional guides with the immeasurable help of my uncle, John Wong. Since a good portion of the translations were poetic and symbolic, the students asked for clarification on many points and many different aspects. Soon through the questions the students asked, I became more and more involved in the philosophy, history, methods and techniques of Tai Chi Chuan. This book is a direct result of all those translations and clarifications.

foreword

To gain proper perspective of Tai Chi Chuan, one must first acquire a total view of the Chinese boxing system more popularly known as kung-fu. Visualize for a moment a spectrum in the form of a rainbow-like half circle. This spectrum represents the whole range of kung-fu schools. The terms "soft fist," "Noi-Kung" and "Mol-Don" designate all schools to the left. The terms "hard fist" and "Shaolin" mark all schools to the right. The schools toward the center incorporate elements from both extremes. Where a school lies on the spectrum depends entirely on the emphasis it places on training methods and techniques. If the training methods stress soft techniques, the school lies somewhere to the left of the spectrum. If the school stresses soft techniques exclusively, it lies to the extreme left. On the other hand, if the training methods stress hard techniques, the school lies somewhere to the right of the spectrum. If the school stresses hard techniques exclusively, it lies to the extreme right. If both hard and soft techniques are emphasized, the school lies either to the left or right of center depending on which training methods are stressed most.

Characteristics distinguishing soft fist schools from hard fist schools are as follows: movements are slow, relaxed, continuous, even and soft; emphasis is on the inward movement of the mind toward quietness, tranquillity and meditativeness; training does not necessarily demand hard physical exertion; conditioning of the hands, feet and striking areas of the body through the use of punching bags, sand bags and bean bags is prohibited.

In contrast, the main characteristics of the hard fist schools are: fast, tense, hard movements; emphasis is on the outgoing mind, competing and sparring with an opponent; training demands great physical exertion; the conditioning of all areas of the body for striking and blocking through the use of punching bags, sand bags and others is a necessary part of the training.

The term "internal" refers to all methods of breathing designed for the sole purpose of developing Chi. "Chi" means vital force, internal power or intrinsic energy. "Internal" refers to the method and "Chi" is the result of the method. "Noi-Kung" literally means inner force, inner strength or internal power, implying both the method and the result. The terms "internal," "Chi" and "Noi-Kung" are sometimes confusing because they are used interchangeably.

Not all hard fist schools practice internal methods, but all soft fist schools do. For all soft fist schools the internal methods are the only means to the cultivation of Chi which is Noi-Kung.

The term "external" refers to all methods and techniques designed to harden and condition the body from a physical standpoint while the internal method stresses a psychophysiological view. All hard and soft fist schools employ external methods. It is their approach to the employment of these methods that determines whether the school is soft or hard.

Chang-San Feng, the legendary martial arts master, is reputedly the father and founder of Tai Chi Chuan. According to legend, he established a monastery on the mountain called Mol-Don. Here he taught his students the centuries-old principles and methods of the soft fist which he synthesized and codified. Whenever the term Mol-Don is mentioned, it is automatically associated with Chang-San Feng and Tai Chi Chuan.

Shaolin is the name of a Buddhist monastery in China which produced fighting monks of great renown. Most of the kung-fu schools surviving today originated from Shaolin although not all hard fist schools have their roots there. Still, because all Shaolin schools employ hard fist methods, Western students of Tai Chi Chuan mistakenly tend to think of Shaolin and hard fist as synonymous terms. The Shaolin schools have endured to this day because their masters, realizing that there is always area for improvement, were open to many other methods and incorporated some of these in their teachings. As the soft fist style and culture began to challenge the hard fist style and culture, these Shaolin masters observed, listened and learned with quiet intelligence. Eventually they adopted as their own those soft fist principles and methods they felt most applicable and effective. To this day, the syntheses of hard and soft methods can be seen in demonstrations put on by the Shaolin schools of the White Crane, the Eagle Claw or the Praying Mantis.

Looking at the spectrum, then, one sees the vastness of the number and range of kung-fu schools. They run from hard-hard to hard, hard to hard-soft, soft-hard to soft, soft to soft-soft. Obviously the variety of schools indicates a comparable range of philosophies. The differences in attitudes and methods of training between hard and soft, external and internal, Shaolin and Mol-Don, lie in the principles and rules derived from these diverse philosophies. It is my intention and purpose to clarify the philosophy and principles of the Art of the Soft Fist.

Tai Chi Chuan, Bak Gwa Chang and Ying Yee Chuan lie at the extreme left of the spectrum, the main branches of the schools of the Soft Fist. In China today, however, Tai Chi Chuan is the most renowned and widely practiced. By clarifying the philosophy and principles of the Art of the Soft Fist, I clarify not only the basis of Tai Chi Chuan, but the basis of Bak Gwa Chang, Ying Yee Chuan, and all other schools utilizing the methods and principles of the Soft Fist (such as the Japanese martial art schools of Judo and Aikido).

To understand the basis of Tai Chi Chuan is to understand its underlying system of fundamental principles. The axioms of the system define and restrict its structural size, arrangement and its functional range. Knowledge of and familiarity with these principles determines the difference between hard and soft, external and internal, Shaolin and Mol-Don: one knows whether one is or is not practicing Tai Chi Chuan properly. Mastery and proficiency in the art come only through understanding these fundamental principles and their application through meditation, health and self-defense.

The criteria for judging the proficiency of both masters and students alike is derived from these fundamental principles. Since the master and student are both products of the system, the same set of criteria determines their competence.

Tai Chi Chuan encompasses many styles: Sak, Mo, Sun, Eng, Yang, Wu and so forth. This book deals with the Yang system—specifically, the Yang system of Tai Chi Chuan as taught by Master Raymond Y.M. Chung of Vancouver, B.C., Canada. My main intention is to outline, describe and explain the structure and composition of the Yang system, its fundamental principles, and the rules related to each unit within the structure. In so doing, I hope to give Western students a more comprehensive view of the art.

Most people associate Tai Chi Chuan with only the solo, empty-hand exercise forms. (Depending on the master, these number anywhere from twenty-four to one hundred and eight or more movements.) Yet, Tai Chi Chuan consists of other forms of practice as well. In the Yang system, besides the solo, empty-hand exercise forms, there exist applications, sparring methods for two people, Join—Stick—Push Hands Practice, sensitivity exercises for two people and solo forms of weaponry practice. These will also be discussed.

This book is designed and written specifically for students of the Yang system of Tai Chi Chuan, but may also benefit all students of the larger Art of the Soft Fist, regardless of their particular branch of study. In the future, I hope to present a more exhaustive study of the other special sections of the Yang system of Tai Chi Chuan.

In closing I wish to state that all schools of meditation and all groups associated with the growth potential movement may greatly benefit from this book, especially those sections on meditation, health, sensitivity, human relationship and the master-pupil relationship. The descriptions of my experiences and the value judgments that I make throughout this book are mine and mine alone. I take full responsibility for them. When I speak with authority, I mean that I speak with the authority of personal passion and personal conviction. It is not the authority of a master. I am not your master. I ask only that we share our knowledge, experiences and understanding when we take that journey in the search for happiness, God or truth.

Douglas R. Lee

mottos

First You Crawl.
Then You Walk.
Then You Run.

Therefore Your MOTTO is:
STILLNESS precedes MOTION.
SLOWNESS precedes SPEED.
SOFTNESS precedes STRENGTH.

Because:
Stillness, Slowness and Softness
are
the
FOUNDATIONS
of
Motion, Speed and Strength

contents

chapter I ——————————————

I. TAI CHI CHUAN

A. A BRIEF HISTORY
B. THE CONCEPT OF YIN-YANG
C. THE MEANING AND RELATIONSHIP OF TAI CHI TO CHUAN
D. TAI CHI CHUAN AND YOGA
E. MEDITATION, THE FIRST BASIC ESSENTIAL ELEMENT
F. HEALTH, THE SECOND BASIC ESSENTIAL ELEMENT
G. SELF-DEFENSE, THE THIRD BASIC ESSENTIAL ELEMENT
H. MEDITATION, HEALTH AND SELF-DEFENSE: CONTRADICTORY AND INCOMPATIBLE?
I. MEDITATION AND SELF-DEFENSE: PRACTICE AND INTEGRATION
J. CHI

I. TAI CHI CHUAN

A. A BRIEF HISTORY

No one knows for sure the exact origins of Tai Chi Chuan. It had, no doubt, many precursors, the most prominent being the Taoist schools. These practiced forms of exercise that combined breathing movements with animal forms. In the Taoist T'ang Dynasty, the *Thirty-Seven Forms, After Birth Method,* and *Fourteen Forms* schools practiced forms of the Soft Fist. It is no wonder many people feel the founder of Tai Chi Chuan derived his method from the Taoist schools. Some feel he derived his method from observing a white stork fight a snake in the mountains. Still others feel he discovered his fist method in a dream.

In my opinion, the founder of Tai Chi Chuan derived his method in manner similar to Jigoro Kano's. Jigoro Kano (1860—1938) was a very famous Japanese martial arts master who, as a young man, studied under several jujitsu schools. When his knowledge became more sophisticated, he took the best methods and techniques from each school, combining, systematizing and codifying these elements. He called the resulting art, Kano Judo. A short time later his system demonstrated its superiority over jujitsu, and the Kodokan was built in his honor. Someone must have done likewise for the Chinese martial arts and founded Tai Chi Chuan. Chang-San Feng is usually credited as this person. No one, however, agrees on the period in which Chang lived. Estimates range anywhere from the eighth to the thirteenth century A.D.

Many stories about Chang-San Feng have been handed down to us through an old Chinese source book called *Nam, Liu, Jack,* a collection of stories about Chang taken from engravings on the tombstones of people who knew of him. According to one of the stories, Chang was living at Mol-Don mountain practicing the art of Chinese alchemy and searching for the elixir of life when the Sung Dynasty emperor Fai Jung decided to ask for his help in bringing law and order to his community. The emperor's courier missed the path to Mol-Don and failed to reach Chang. Chang, however, dreamed that the emperor preceding Fai Jung had shown him the fist method. This made it possible for him to come alone out of the mountains and kill over one hundred bandits who had been threatening the citizens of that area.

Another story described Chang as a dirty dresser with an unkempt beard and long hair piled into a bun. He had a large stomach, a deep, red face, and wore a bamboo hat. No matter what time of the year it was, he always dressed in the same thin gown.

His eating habits were like an animal's. When there was food he would devour it ravenously and when there was none he could go without it for several days. He could walk a thousand days continuously at a fast and quick pace. He was playful and naughty. Unlike other masters who were always serious, he played with his students at the Mol-Don monastery. For his wild dress and wooly manners they named him dirty, old Chang.

According to others Chang was quite tall, handsome and broadly built. He was shaped like a tortoise and a crane to an extraordinary degree, with large ears and round eyes. His moustache and beard, however, were like those of a ruffian.

Chang-San Feng's foremost pupil was Wang Tsung-yueh. No one knows exactly when Wang lived. Anywhere from the twelfth to sixteenth century A.D., Wang is said to have taught his boxing method to Chen Chia Kou in Wen-hsien of Honan. This Chen family supposedly held the secret of Tai Chi Chuan for over four hundred years. Later the Chen group split into two groups: the old and the new. Yang Lu Chan (1798—1872), the great-grandfather of the Yang system of Tai Chi Chuan, learned the old system from Chen Chang Hsing. Yang developed Tai Chi Chuan to its highest pinnacle. He passed on his art to his two sons Yang Pan Hou and Yang Chien Hou (1839—1917). Then Yang Chien Hou passed the art down through his two sons Yang Shao Hou (1862—1929) and Yang Cheng Fu (1883—1936). It was Yang Cheng Fu's teachings which made it possible for Tai Chi Chuan to spread to south China and overseas. In recognition of his accomplishments, the Yang school of Tai Chi Chuan was named after him. His son Yang Shou Chung, who now lives and teaches in Hong Kong, is carrying on the tradition. It is through the efforts of Yang Cheng Fu, his sons and students that the Yang system of Tai Chi Chuan has survived both in China and throughout the rest of the world.

B. THE CONCEPT OF YIN—YANG

Symbol

The Yin-Yang symbol is a circle divided, by a serpentine line, into two equal parts which form two fish-like figures curving into each other. One half of the area is white and the other is black. Within the white area is a small black circle. Within the black area is a small white circle.

Concept

The Yin, the black area of the circle, can represent anything in the universe as female, passive, negative, night or soft. The Yang, the white area of the circle, represents the opposite as male, active, positive, day or hard. At first glance, Yin and Yang seem to be pairs of opposites that are dualistic, contentive and conflictive. If one looks closer, one can see that the line dividing the two areas is not straight, but serpentine. That curved line signifies the flow and eventual synthesis of one area into the other. The black spot in the white area and the white spot in the black area indicate that everything includes its own opposite and that nothing can be so completely itself that it does not contain something of its opposite.

Yin and Yang are a pair of complementary forces that act in the universe unceasingly. They indicate that everything appears to be one-half of a pair of opposites: left and right, up and down, forward and backward, yet it is impossible to have one without the other. The balance between opposites indicates their essential interdependence and the existence of a common ground upon which they stand. This common bond is the circle, representing the whole that contains and gives birth to the parts: Yin and Yang. This whole is Tai Chi.

C. THE MEANING AND RELATIONSHIP OF TAI CHI TO CHUAN

Tai Chi Chuan represents a fusion of spiritual culture with physical culture. Spiritually, it incorporates the Taoist principle of non-doing with the Buddhist principle of serenity. Physically, it utilizes the principle of health based on the strengthening and relaxing of the whole human body.

Tai Chi is the Grand Ultimate. It is the beginning and the end. It is the timeless, the infinite, the eternal. Tai Chi is reality, truth, God or whatever one wishes to call it.

Chuan literally means fist. A fist normally conjures thoughts of pugilism and the like. Chuan represents the total physical man. The practice of Chuan is the development of the complete man physically in terms of a whole physical culture.

The practice of Tai Chi Chuan is the practice of a complete physical culture. Its purpose is to use Chuan as a vehicle for experiencing Tai Chi, the Grand Ultimate; and so the system is named.

D. TAI CHI CHUAN AND YOGA

There are many similarities and differences between Tai Chi Chuan and Yoga. The similarities lie in three main areas. First, their methods are designed for meditation, for self-awareness and for enlightenment. Second, they both stress good breathing techniques based around the psychic navel center, tandem or *hara*. Third, they both stress softness, pliability and total relaxation as essential techniques to attain *satori*. In essence their systems are designed to bring the mind and body into harmony by making them one.

To develop pliability and softness in Yoga, special exercises have been developed. One takes a form or posture and holds that posture as long as possible. During this time one concentrates on one's breathing. Concentration on the movement and flow of breathing integrates and brings all the different biorhythms of the body into harmony. Good breathing techniques lead to good biorhythms. Good biorhythms integrate body and mind. This harmony relaxes the mind and the body and brings peace.

To develop softness and pliability in Tai Chi Chuan, one enters a form through slow movement, goes through the form, then slowly leaves the form and continues without stopping, going likewise through a series of forms and postures until the whole set is completed. It is like a rubber band being pulled taut and then slowly released and pulled taut and released again. This method is Tai Chi Chuan's principal technique.

Unlike Yoga which uses breathing techniques to bring about good biorhythms, Tai Chi Chuan uses its flowing movements to create good biorhythms which produce good breathing naturally. Good runners, for example, develop a running rhythm which makes possible the coordination of all body movements with breathing. This integration makes running effortless. Developing good biorhythms by maintaining continuous motion, and by never holding a static position is the principal factor distinguishing Tai Chi Chuan from Yoga. Therefore, Yoga is said to be internal activity creating external serenity, while Tai Chi Chuan is external activity engendering internal tranquillity.

E. MEDITATION, THE FIRST
BASIC ESSENTIAL ELEMENT

In the beginning we come out of the world. At that time we are barely aware of the world around us. It is not I who am aware of the world. There is no I, no me, no self. There is only awareness. There is no center from which to be aware.

A newborn baby does not develop ego-consciousness at once. Eventually he has many experiences and as these experiences are thought over, related and evaluated, the thinker, the experiencer, the self is born. Thought creates a feeling of the center which in turn becomes the self, the I, the me, the sense of ego.

The self is this accumulation of knowledge and experiences. In essence the self is all that is known. The known is the past. If you can think of a past, you can think of a future. The past and the future create time. The self therefore is time. If there were no memory, no thought, there would be no time and no self. The self is always bound and limited within the realm of time and the known. Time cannot know the timeless, but the timeless contains time. The finite cannot grasp the infinite, but the infinite contains the finite. The limits cannot contain the limitless, but the limitless encloses the limits. For the self to seek, to desire or to attain the timeless, the unknown, truth, reality or God is futile. The timeless, the unknown, the eternal will be, when the self is not. This knowledge and understanding of the self is the beginning of meditation.

Meditation is a revealing approach to the understanding of the ways of the self, its aims, its intentions, its purposes, its desires, its beliefs, its thought and its pursuits. The self has built around itself a wall of knowledge, experiences, beliefs and ideals to give itself permanency, security and fulfillment. Meditation breaks down this wall. Once the wall is broken down, you are free to step beyond it and enter the river of life. Moving with it with no resistance is to be completely open, sensitive and vulnerable. Meditation is this state of freedom, openness, sensitivity and vulnerability.

Meditation is not a means to an end. It is definitely not a path to truth, reality or God. A path can only lead you to a fixed point. The fixed point is the past. Life is movement. How can there be a path or road to what is always in motion?

The meditator may control his thoughts, discipline them, guide them and have his results. Since the meditator and the self are one, these results can only lead to self-fulfillment. Why take such a difficult road? There are easier methods to thought control. All you have to do is take a drug and it is accomplished. Is the result, is this experience, meditation?

What can be made, can be unmade. Thought can be made and therefore thought can be unmade. Thought is always within the confinement of time, because thought is time. When thought is not, is there time? When thought is not, then the meditator is not. When the meditator is not, then meditation is the timeless.

Tai Chi Chuan is a system with many methods and techniques. It does not teach a method of meditation. What it does do is to help you to know and discover yourself. Knowledge of yourself is the beginning of meditation. The senses that you use to be aware of the world around you are the same senses that you use to be aware of yourself. The solo and partner patterns of movement in Tai Chi Chuan are a test to find out how sensitive and aware you are to yourself. In the solo movements you are testing to see if you are aware of your own body in relation to the positions of form. If you do have good body awareness, it implies you have good kinesthetic perception. It means you are able to perform the movements quite well.

Society is man's relationship to man. The Art of Join—Stick—Push Hands tests the sensitivity between two persons. It tests to see if each one has the proper attitude and proper approach in relationships. Push Hands practice cannot be performed correctly if either partner has an incorrect attitude. Meditation embodies the proper attitude and the correct approach to life. Tai Chi Chuan is meditation only to the extent that it helps you to come to know and understand the attitude of yourself to yourself in relationship to others.

F. HEALTH, THE SECOND
BASIC ESSENTIAL ELEMENT

Good health may be perceived on two different levels: the mind and the body. The mind influences the body as much as the body influences the mind. Psychosomatic illnesses such as ulcer, asthma and colitis are examples of the bad effects of the mind on the body. A strong, robust body always has its good effects on the mind. When the mind and the body are in harmony, good health results.

Tai Chi Chuan is divided into several levels of training. On the first level the training is done gently, slowly and softly. As you continue, the training becomes progressively more intense and vigorous. For elderly people who are out of condition and for people who have heart conditions or the like, Tai Chi Chuan teaching is an excellent system for getting back into condition.

Because Tai Chi is practiced softly, slowly and gently, it has a splendid relaxation potential. For people who suffer from psychosomatic illnesses and hypertension, and for normal people who lead tense lives because of constant pressure, the practice of Tai Chi can be beneficial.

People take up all kinds of physical exercises to get into shape. Yet many quit before it has done them enough good. The factor of motivation is the strength of Tai Chi Chuan. All the exercises in Tai Chi Chuan are such that you must have intense concentration before the movements can be done properly.

Scientific research in the fields of physiology and kinesiology has shown that endurance exercises are the only exercises that can help build up our respiratory and cardiovascular systems. Endurance exercises by strengthening the respiratory and cardiovascular system can help to ward off heart attacks and lung diseases.

Endurance exercises require great physical exertion. Only in the Walking Join—Stick—Push Hands phase of Tai Chi Chuan does one exert oneself to this degree. Unfortunately, many practitioners of the art do not know this phase of Tai Chi. Tai Chi Chuan as a total system is beneficial for health by teaching methods that stress the training and conditioning of both mind and body equally.

G. SELF-DEFENSE, THE THIRD
BASIC ESSENTIAL ELEMENT

Many Westerners know Tai Chi only as a health exercise. They do not know that it is also a martial art. Tai Chi Chuan as a system of self-defense has proved itself many times. The attitude toward others, the training procedures and methods, the stages of training distinguish Tai Chi Chuan's approach from the hard schools' approach to self-defense.

In its attitude toward life and living Tai Chi Chuan differs immeasurably from the hard fist schools. When someone attacks a Tai Chi Chuan practitioner, his view is as follows: the person who attacks me is a living human being. He exudes life force. When he attacks me, it is his life force that is concentrated and swiftly bearing down on me. Life force does not oppose life force; therefore, I do not oppose the attacker's force. Those who love do not destroy. So I step aside and permit the attacker's life force to pass through. As he comes flying by, I give him a nudge to help him to get where he is going more quickly. That is the attitude with which all students of the Soft Fist should approach others.

In its training procedures and methods Tai Chi Chuan differs greatly from the hard fist schools. All phases of the training must be mastered by first practicing them slowly, softly and with complete relaxation. Hard fist schools employ dynamic tension techniques, speed and power right from the beginning of the training. The Tai Chi Chuan student may later learn to apply the techniques with speed and power, but must still be able to remain relatively relaxed. In the pushing hands section the student must maintain his soft touch even though he may be moving extremely fast.

Hard schools such as Wing Chun have a pushing hands section too, but the flow is fast, powerful and hard. Tai Chi pushing hands can be either slow or fast, but it is always soft. All blocking action in the pushing hands, *Ta Lu*, and application sections should be soft. The blocking hand or arm should feel hardly any resistance to any incoming force. All self-defense techniques should be executed and completed in one continuous flow.

In learning the system of self-defense in Tai Chi Chuan the student must progress through five stages of training. The first stage requires the student to practice his breathing while sitting in a moving straddle leg stance to develop both physical strength and Chi, that vital force that gives Tai Chi masters such exceptional mental and physical powers and robust health.

The second stage requires the student to learn the solo, formal exercise that varies in length from one Tai Chi school to another. The solo exercise teaches the student balance in motion, basic striking and soft parrying techniques and basic principles of softness. The third stage requires the student to learn the pushing hands exercise which teaches the student balance against an opponent, sensitivity of touch, timing and distance appreciation. The fourth stage requires the student to learn the 88 movements which is an integrated pattern of attack and defense applying all the knowledge and techniques acquired from the first three stages. The fifth stage requires the student to integrate and intermix all the patterns he has learned from the first four stages, so that he can flow spontaneously from one pattern to another and from one form to another. The goal is for the student to be able to defend himself competently and efficiently according to the principle of softness upon which the system is based.

H. MEDITATION, HEALTH AND SELF-DEFENSE: CONTRADICTORY AND INCOMPATIBLE?

Meditation, health and self-defense seem contradictory and incompatible, but nothing could be further from the truth. The practice of all three involves the training of both mind and body.

In meditation the mind is very much involved with the body. When the mind is disturbed, the body is disturbed. Mental conflict is reflected in muscle tension and tightness. It is also true that the physical state affects the mental state. In meditation, learning to relax the body helps to relax the mind and to make the mind tranquil. In this type of biofeedback the mind uses the body as a mirror reflecting itself. In this state the mind is more receptive.

Self-defense is like meditation. It requires that one become aware of one's own body; otherwise, one would not be able to defend oneself from physical harm. The body must be conditioned to become flexible and strong. A mind and body in harmony deny contradiction and incompatibility.

I. MEDITATION AND SELF-DEFENSE: PRACTICE AND INTEGRATION

People sometimes argue that Tai Chi Chuan is meditation and not self-defense and vice versa, but both views are wrong. Tai Chi Chuan is both meditation and self-defense at the same time; the system is designed so that the two are inseparable. When you are practicing one, you are practicing the other.

System implies structure. Structure implies form. All the

physical forms in Tai Chi Chuan are based on self-defense forms, expressing its martial arts origin. Self-defense forms are predicated on the principles of kinesiology: of balance and body mechanics. The movements from form to form express the meditative attitude and approach in physical terms. In all phases of Tai Chi Chuan training the practices of meditation and self-defense are intertwined.

J. CHI

Chi is not quite life force. It is an aspect of life force. It is intrinsic energy, inner power, a vital force that is inherent in all human beings. Once this vital force is released in the individual it is supposed to bring him robust health, strength and longevity. For the schools of meditation such as Zen and Yoga, Chi brings enlightenment. For all the Chinese internal boxing schools the power that Chi brings is applied not only for meditation and enlightenment but also for health and self-defense.

The principal technique for the development and cultivation of Chi in Tai Chi Chuan is in the practice of Tai Chi Chuan's 82 movements, sometimes referred to as the 108 movements. Unless the 82 movements are practiced properly the cultivation of Chi is not possible. The combination of relaxation and proper breathing within the movements is the key to Chi. One is to bring one's breath into a circular flow traveling from a point beginning three inches below the navel (referred to as the psychic navel center), up one's back to the brain, down one's front to the point of origin. Along this circular path lie 12 centers. Each of these centers acts as a filter. As each breath makes its cycle each time, it purifies itself more and more until breath becomes Chi. Chi is then stored at the psychic navel center. Because breath is purified by traveling through lungs, blood and mind, Chi is sometimes defined as the psychophysical energy associated with breath, blood and mind.

A parallel to Chi in the Western world is the power released through self-hypnosis, which has been used to counteract pain in childbirth and to replace anaesthetic drugs in operations. In self-hypnosis and in Tai Chi Chuan it is the technique of relaxation that releases this mysterious power.

Chi may or may not result in enlightenment or good health. There is no doubt that Chi is energy. This energy is power.

■

chapter II

II. GENERAL PRINCIPLES AND RULES

A. PSYCHO-PHYSICAL RELATIONSHIP = THE ELEVEN KEY
   POINTS
   (MIND-BODY RELATIONSHIP)
   1. Be Soft (Relax)
   2. Be Slow
   3. Be Non-Aggressive
   4. Be Natural (Spontaneous)
   5. Be Sensitive
   6. Be Moderate (Avoid Extremes)
   7. Be Always In Motion (Flow)
   8. Maintain Continuity
   9. Be Timeless
   10. Be Attentive (Alert, Aware)
   11. Harmonize
B. PHYSICAL PRINCIPLES AND RULES: BALANCE AND
   BODY MECHANICS
C. BREATHING METHODS AND RULES

II. GENERAL PRINCIPLES AND RULES

A. PSYCHO-PHYSICAL RELATIONSHIP
= THE ELEVEN KEY POINTS
(MIND-BODY RELATIONSHIP)

A CLARIFICATION OF THE ELEVEN KEY POINTS

1. BE SOFT (RELAX)

To be soft is to relax, to yield. Softness serves five major purposes:

(1) The Promotion of Muscle Pliability and Flexibility

Every muscle of the body is in a state of permanent, partial tension, even during rest. This persistent continuous tension is called muscle tone or tonus. The performance of any exercise requires the exertion of force and a corresponding increase in tension. This force or tension comes about naturally from the contraction of the muscles. For each contraction there must be complete muscle relaxation, otherwise residual tension remains, builds up, constricts and hampers muscle flexibility. Then movements become jerky, inhibited and awkward. If there is complete relaxation for every contraction, movement will be free, smooth and flowing. Softness gives immense mobility. Remember to do all exercises SOFTLY.

(2) Minimum Effort For Maximum Result

Softness promotes Efficiency. If you are tense all the time, you will be exerting force continually and this means expending an enormous amount of energy. To use only those muscles required to perform a particular act and not to use other muscles is to be efficient. You must learn to relax, to conserve energy and to utilize it more efficiently by expending only the amount really needed. In this way Softness will promote greater Efficiency.

(3) The Improvement of the Function of the Respiratory and Circulatory System

Softness improves the function of the respiratory system. Hardness impedes its function by preventing the diaphragm and other respiratory muscles from becoming flexible. To be soft is to have efficient muscles which promotes muscle flexibility.

Softness improves the function and tone of the circulatory system by making the respiratory and skeletal muscles contract more efficiently. This aids the return of venous blood to the heart by increasing the pressure gradient between peripheral veins and the vena cava.

Respiration increases the pressure gradient between peripheral and central veins. Every time the diaphragm contracts the thoracic cavity expands and the abdominal cavity contracts. Thoracic cavity pressure decreases as abdominal cavity pressure increases.

(4) The Avoidance of Anxiety

Softness alleviates anxiety. It is extremely difficult to be anxious if relaxed.

(5) The Development of Clear Thinking

Softness also aids clear thinking. It is very difficult not to become overly emotional during times of crisis. As long as the mind is in a distressed emotional state, it is disorderly and confused. Only when it is calm and quiet can the mind become receptive and responsive. Only then can a mind be called soft (relaxed). Only clear thinking can handle and cope with anxious moments and situations as they arise.

Relaxation is a physical state but it is under the control of the mind. Relaxation is acquired by the conscious effort to control one's thought as well as action patterns. In acquiring relaxation it takes perception, practice and willingness to train the mind into new habits of thinking and the body into new habits of action. Complete habitual relaxation with no unnecessary tension is improbable for most individuals, but the ability to relax the body voluntarily, even occasionally, is an accomplishment well worth the time, effort and practice involved.

In the beginning you will find that you will use the mental state to control the physical state in order to relax. In the latter stages you will find that true relaxation has nothing whatsoever to do with the mental state controlling the physical state. The mind must literally let go. All effort, all thought, all desire prevents mental and physical relaxation. It is only when one acts without conscious thought, without apparent effort that one is truly relaxed. In that effortlessness lies spontaneity, the heart of real relaxation.

2. BE SLOW

Do the formal calisthenics (Tai Chi's 82) slowly. Slowness serves seven purposes:

(1) It gives the beginner time to think; that is, time to concentrate on the execution of each form (technique) as he does it.

(2) It forces the student to give his complete attention to each form as he does it; otherwise his attention becomes fragmented and his forms completely break down.

(3) It prevents damage to muscle tissues from sudden exertion. It gives the muscles time to warm up.

(4) It makes it easier for the instructor to notice and correct the errors that the student makes in the execution of each form.

(5) It prevents the student from using his momentum to help him, for example when turning on one foot. By being slow the student is forced to use every necessary muscle to execute each form.

(6) It teaches good body balance through muscle control and coordination. It develops kinesthetic perception.
    a. KINESTHETIC PERCEPTION is the ability to feel muscles contract and relax, to know what a muscle is doing. It is also the ability to feel and to know the position of every muscle and bone while in motion.

(7) It prevents a person from becoming hard (building residual tension). It is very difficult to be soft and relaxed when doing something fast.

Every individual has his own natural, normal tempo. In a culture such as ours we become conditioned to a faster tempo than our forefathers. Tai Chi helps to decondition us from this fast moving pace and find our own individual tempos.

In the beginning you will notice yourself tensing up if you rise above or go below your own normal pace while exercising. It is only through constant awareness of the tension and constant practice of going at a slightly slower tempo that you can bring your tempo down. Eventually you will be able to be relaxed even at an extremely slow tempo. In the advanced stages you will be able to maintain perfect control and coordination whether moving rapidly or slowly.

3. BE NON-AGGRESSIVE

You cannot *try* to be non-aggressive. You can only *be* non-aggressive. Trying to be and being are not the same thing. When you try to be, it implies that you are *this* and you wish to become *that*. While you are trying, you are still in an aggressive state.

In understanding non-aggression you must first understand aggression—how it came into being and why. Non-aggression cannot be desired, because desire *is* aggression. Aggression comes about when the self feels empty and lonely. These feelings create fear. The first step in overcoming fear is to see what *you* are at this moment. (Trying to become what you should be, what you want to be, is merely an escape.) The struggle to be what you wish to be, the conflict between what you are and what you wish to be, creates anxiety or pain.

Your possessions, both psychological and material, give you security. This attachment to ideas, to things, to people is a source of pain. You are not separate from your loneliness, emptiness, fear and pain. You *are* these things. *Only by understanding this whole process can you know the meaning of non-aggression.*

When you are exercising and going through the motions of striking and blocking in the formal calisthenics (Tai Chi's 82) do not focus your mind on what you are doing or you will tense your muscles excessively. All you would be doing is going through the motions. You do not need to focus.

Non-aggression does not mean passivity. It does not mean that you permit yourself to be attacked without defending yourself. It does mean that you will not even think of attacking or harming anyone. Externally you will look quite composed. Internally your mind will be alert, open, responsive and receptive, always aware of everything that is happening around you.

Non-aggression is established on a defensive principle. The logic of the principle is that if you do not try to oppose anyone or try to hurt anyone, no one will try to hurt you. The principle is applied to your exercises through the technique of advance and retreat. If your opponent advances, you retreat. If he retreats, you advance. You stick to and follow him, wherever he goes. Advance and retreat, left and right, forward and backward, up and down, hard and soft, all represent motion from one side to the other, stressing a balance of opposites. One side follows and then succeeds the other. From the circle (Tai Chi) of Yin and Yang, female and male, soft and hard arises the principle of no struggle, no conflict, only union, harmony.

4. BE NATURAL (SPONTANEOUS)

In Tai Chi every movement should be comfortable. If it is not, it is wrong. The limbs should never be held stiff and straight. They should always be slightly bent at the joints, with all the joints forming natural curves.

Breathing should never be forced. To force it would be to tense your chest muscles and make your breathing hard. If it is hard (creating residual tension), then you will not feel relaxed after exercising as you should, you will feel tired. Breathing should be done naturally and easily through the nose.

A conditioned mind cannot be natural or spontaneous. Only a free mind can be natural or spontaneous. *A free mind can exist only through the understanding of what a conditioned mind is.* You must understand the structure of the mind completely. Then you will know its function and its limitations and you will understand what a conditioned mind is. A conditioned mind cannot comprehend itself because it is prejudiced and closed. Only an open mind can be free and unprejudiced.

Your whole cultural heritage, political, social, religious, economic and scientific, has conditioned your mind, has shaped it to conform to all past knowledge. A conditioned mind can only act according to its own conditioning, according to its past heritage, according to what is known. All conditioned responses are old. This conditioning restricts you and confines you to the dictates of the past. As long as memory, thought and the past act in the present, you can never be free to respond spontaneously to the present moment. Freedom is spontaneity. Spontaneity is without preconceived thought patterns.

All thinking and all motion should be natural and spontaneous. There should be no conceptual reflecting, no cogitating. Everything should be automatic. Spontaneity comes about only through understanding of the role that technique or method plays in the totality. Technique or method is only a part. When you can understand the value that the part plays in the totality of mastering Tai Chi, then you will have gone beyond technique and method. You will be spontaneous and natural. You will have perfection of method without apparent method. Outer form and inner significance will have merged into one unified whole.

5. BE SENSITIVE

You respond to the present through the screen of the past. The screen of past thoughts and emotions often prevents you from seeing clearly. Because your seeing is fragmented, your response is also fragmented. That produces sentimentality. To be sensitive is to see everything instantly and objectively, and to relate to the whole past simultaneously so that the action and the response are one—complete and inseparable.

Sensitivity, then, has nothing to do with being sentimental or emotional. It has to do with a state of simplicity, a state of awareness. As long as the mind is burdened with beliefs and opinions it cannot be sensitive. All knowledge and belief are loaded with prejudices and desires. As long as your mind is conditioned by all that, you cannot approach anything new without absorbing the new through the old. When you realize this, then the screen of preconceived ideas and notions can begin to dissolve. Sensitivity is the awareness of all internal and external stimuli. It means that, through your sensory perceptions, you can respond wholly and automatically to any imminent danger.

In the practice of physical culture you work to develop two main perceptions: the sensitivity of touch and of feeling. It is through one organ, the skin, that you concentrate your development of touch. But it is through the development of the total organism, the human body, that you concentrate your development of feeling. The human body, as a totality, is sensitive to such things as temperature and pressure, both internal and external.

Although you concentrate on the use of these two senses for self-defense purposes, you must not neglect to use all the other senses if you wish for a balanced awareness of your surroundings in the practice and perfection of the art of Tai Chi Chuan.

6. BE MODERATE (AVOID EXTREMES)

The application of the principle of moderation in the Tai Chi formal calisthenics is accomplished in three ways:

(1) Never step as far as possible.
(2) Never extend the arms as far as possible.
    (Don't lock your joints.)
(3) Reserve a part of the end of each movement for the beginning of the next one.

From an empirical standpoint, the understanding drawn from the application of the principle of moderation in the Tai Chi calisthenics cannot help but influence the attitudes taken in the execution of the formal exercise.

Yin includes some Yang; Yang includes some Yin. Everything includes some attribute of its opposite. The Tai Chi symbol represents the principle of moderation, which when practiced and applied in the formal calisthenics gives a feeling of wholeness, unity and oneness.

7. BE ALWAYS IN MOTION (FLOW)

Taoistic philosophy takes the view that life is impermanent. It is forever changing, forever transforming, forever flowing. Life is never static. Whatever is static is dead.

Adequate muscle tone and a well-balanced interplay of tension and release are usually associated with general well-being and emotional stability. From motion you obtain serenity and stability by the release of tension through the continuous shifting of weight from one foot to the other. It is through this shifting that one side of the body becomes soft (muscles relaxed) and the other side hard (muscles contracted). As a result of these skeletal muscle contractions, circulation is improved and the person feels relaxed and not fatigued.

8. MAINTAIN CONTINUITY

From its beginning to the present time, Chinese civilization has maintained its continuity through its culture. The principle of continuity is applied in the formal calisthenics in three ways:

(1) The same tempo is maintained throughout each movement.
(2) From the beginning to the end there should be no break. The significance of this is explained by the story of the cocoon of a silkworm. If you were to draw out a thread from the cocoon of a silkworm you would not pull it out quickly and then slowly, because the thread would easily break. If the thread were withdrawn smoothly and evenly it would emerge uniform and strong.
(3) The beginning is the end; the end is the beginning. That is the circle and the cycle of nature.

In formal calisthenics you should finish in exactly the same position as you started. By so doing you return to the beginning, to your origin; you complete the circle and cycle of life.

Remember that uniform tempo and speed in Tai Chi's 82 positions contributes to an even flow, thereby preventing any breaks, and aiding the continuity of the Whole.

9. BE TIMELESS

Time is memory. Memory is time. If you can think of a past you can think of a future. The future is merely a projection of the past. The present is merely a passage to the future.

Time implies becoming. You are *this* and you want to become *that*. You have only *these*, but you also want *those*.

Memory created thought. Without thought there is no memory, no time. Thought gives memory *continuity* in time. Thought is time. Time is *continuity*.

If you do not give your complete attention to each movement as it arises in your exercises, they will all become boring and tedious, sloppy and careless. You must not think about what you have just done or what you are about to do; otherwise, these thoughts will fragment your attention. Fragmentation divides the mind and wastes the energy you need for attention. You must "die" totally to each form as it is completed. If you can let go of the past completely, then you can pay attention to what you are doing now at this moment and the present will ever be fresh and new. When you understand that the *beginning is the end and the end is the beginning*, then all is *timeless and eternal*.

10. BE ATTENTIVE (ALERT, AWARE)

Attentiveness has nothing to do with concentration. Concentration is exclusive attention. This exclusiveness, this focussed awareness, is resistance and requires great effort. It implies that the mind is distracted and that is why one must use effort to overcome the distraction. But effort dissipates energy. If energy is dissipated, how can the mind gather all its energy to be attentive? Attention is complete when the mind is not distracted and fragmented.

Attention gives the mental connection to a physical exercise. Attention is integration of the mind and the body. Control over voluntary muscles is natural and spontaneous. Attention encompasses concentration, but concentration does not encompass attention. By understanding the difference between attention and concentration, one will know the part that each plays in the performance of the formal calisthenics.

Use the peripheral vision of the mind and not its central vision. When you look at any object, you do not see it out of only the corners of your eyes, but with totally attuned attention. When you are sparring, you learn not to over-concentrate. In other words, you learn to use your peripheral vision; otherwise, you will see only the hands of your opponent and not his whole body.

(1) An Illustration Of Faulty Concentration

I dare you to run down, or even walk quickly down a steep flight of stairs by concentrating on each step you make. In all probability you will fall down the stairs. Remember, never go to extremes, don't over-concentrate.

(2) Attention Equals Spontaneity Equals Harmony

In perfect attention everything is done naturally. Because everything is done spontaneously, a union of the mind and the body occurs. The mind is the body. The body is the mind. They are inseparable. We will now consider the importance of this unity.

(3) Integration Of Mind And Body

When one is reading a book and becomes totally absorbed in it, one is exercising in a special way. The mental aspects involved are as follows: (1) The reader is not aware of anything that is happening around him. He does not see, feel or hear anything but what he is reading. (2) He does not say to himself that he is reading. Do you say to yourself when you are absorbed in a fascinating book, "I am reading, I am reading," as you read the book? (3) The reader does not analyze or reflect on what he is doing at that moment. He just does it. He just reads. He does it automatically, naturally and spontaneously.

The physical aspects of this type of exercise are: (1) His eyes run across, up and down the pages. (2) He flips the pages over as he is reading along. (3) He doesn't say to himself, "My eyes are now looking across the page; my eyes are now looking down the page; I am now flipping the pages." All the physical things are done automatically, naturally and spontaneously, without reflection.

When the mind does not think about what it is doing then everything is done quite readily, without any delay or doubt.

(4) Intelligence

Use your mind, not your strength. Intelligence, ingenuity and skill can overcome brute force. Use soft to overcome hard. Never use hard against hard.

(5) Brains Over Brawn: The Story of the Bull

In the vast rolling plains of central China there was a massive Bull that had to be moved to another farm. In order to move him, a group of men had tied up the Bull with ropes and had tried to drag him over to the other farm, but the Bull was just too heavy to move. A clever young lad passing by went over to the group and told them he could easily move the Bull over to the other farm if they would let him do it his way. The group laughed at him but decided that since they were unable to do it themselves, they would let the boy try. At least, they thought, they would all get a laugh out of it. The boy proceeded by first sticking a large brass ring through the Bull's nose. Then he tied a piece of rope to the brass ring. Then he released the ropes that the men had placed around the Bull. With the rope in one hand and the brass ring at the other end, the young lad led the Bull over to the other farm.

The boy had the last laugh. He knew the secret of true strength. It lay not in the brute exertion of the *physical* but in the apparently effortless exertion of the *mental*.

11. HARMONIZE

Life is consciousness. But the mind of man divides the world, categorizes it. He is a part of the world, the culture. In fact he is the epitome, the microcosm of his culture. All the values of his culture are internalized in him. The classification becomes the reality of his world. The word, the symbol, the image in his perceived world is all important. Man is no longer important. The human being becomes only a thing. But reality is not an image, a symbol, a word. It is more than this. Reality is everything. It is all of life: animate and inanimate, cultural and environmental, abstract and concrete, chemical and biological, mental and physical.

If you are not a whole person but a fragmented person, problems in life may be insurmountable. The responses to all the challenges of life are therefore partial and incomplete. This incompleteness is a route to disaster.

If you were a completely integrated person, you would be a *whole* person; wherever you would go and whatever challenges would confront you, you would be able to resolve.

Now you can see that a whole person has an integrated mind: a mind that is totally open. Whenever such a mind faces any decision in life, his response to it is total. He sees that his decision on that part of life, on that particular challenge, is placed in its proper perspective in relation to the whole; and therefore, gives that part its full value. That is the importance of being an integrated person. An integrated human being is truly harmonized.

If you follow the preceding 11 rules and principles diligently, then you will understand what harmony is. Harmony has wholeness and unity. Union has no division. If there is no division, there is no struggle, no conflict. The softness, lightness, gracefulness and the perfect coordination of all movements reflect the thorough integration of the mind and the body. This integration harmonizes you with the universe and gives you peace.

B. PHYSICAL PRINCIPLES AND RULES:
BALANCE AND BODY MECHANICS

1. Footwork
   (1) Stepping
       Always lift the feet. Never drag them.
   (2) Stepping and Turning
       Keep the feet as close to the floor as possible.
   (3) Stepping and Placement
       Be sure that you have firmly established all the weight on one foot before stepping out with the other.
   (4) Placement
       Feet should be placed coming down heel first on forward movements and toe first on backward steps, except where specially noted to the contrary.

       As you place the feet down, pay particular attention to the direction in which the toes point.

2. Keep the shoulders and hips level and the torso perpendicular to the floor as you twist and turn.
3. Maintain an erect posture. The head, neck and spine should form a line that is perpendicular to the floor.
4. Do not permit the knees to extend beyond the toes of their feet. One loses one's balance if one's center of gravity extends beyond its base of support.
5. Do not lock any joints of the body. If a joint is in a safe position for the body it must be able to give in any direction in order to absorb the force of an unexpected blow.
6. A wide stance results in a lower center of gravity and a wide base of support. It increases stability, but decreases mobility. A narrow stance results in a high center of gravity and a small base of support. It decreases stability, but increases mobility. Either is desirable depending upon the circumstances.
7. The thigh muscles are the strongest set of muscles in the human body. Utilize the power of these muscles by concentrating all movements around and through the turning of the hips and waist.
8. For maximum effect when turning, twist the whole torso as a unit, not in isolated parts.
9. If the body is subjected to pushes, pulls or blows with a strong horizontal component, greater stability is obtained if the feet

are separated in a stance parallel to the direction of the line of force.

10. Do not neglect head and eye movements. They should face straight into the direction you move. Remember that the head leads and the rest of the body follows.

11. Arms and hands usually describe a circle or part of a circle (an arc) through any number of planes: horizontal, vertical, frontal or coronal.

C. BREATHING METHODS AND RULES

1. Breathe through the nose.

2. When you are breathing in, expand your abdomen.

   When you are breathing out, relax.

   Center your breathing around your tandem (the point two inches below your navel).

3. Rules of Breathing with Movement:

(1)	Raise Arms	—	Breathe in
	Lower Arms	—	Breathe out
(2)	Open Arms	—	Breathe in
	Close Arms	—	Breathe out
(3)	Push Out	—	Breathe out
	Pull In	—	Breathe in
(4)	Strike Out	—	Breathe out
	Withdraw	—	Breathe in
(5)	Kick	—	Breathe in

4. Deep Breathing and Diaphragm
   The diaphragm is a peculiar muscle because there is no way to exercise it except by breathing. Unless it functions properly deep breathing is impossible. Proper muscular relaxation is the technique to help remove all obstacles that prevent the diaphragm from functioning well.

5. Do not force breathing to fit into form and movement. Form and movement must follow the rhythm of breathing and not vice versa.

6. Do not force breathing at any time. The human body is so perfectly synchronized that the need for oxygen in the body

cells and the rate of delivery by the respiratory and cardiovascular system to these cells is automatically regulated. The two main problems created by unnatural, forced breathing result in (a) Hyperventilation and (b) Hypoventilation. Hyperventilation is forced, rapid and deep breathing which results in the decrease of carbon dioxide in the blood, resulting in an acid-base upset in the body's biochemistry. Hypoventilation is forced, rapid and shallow breathing which results in a lack of oxygen in the blood. In both cases the balance of oxygen and carbon dioxide necessary to the normal functioning of the human body is upset. This biochemical imbalance deprives the brain of oxygen, causing dizziness, weakness and sometimes the tingling of both hands and feet.

■

chapter III_____

III. TAI CHI CHUAN'S SOLO EXERCISES

A. THE APPROACHES TO PRACTICE
B. PHILOSOPHICAL SIGNIFICANCE
C. TAI CHI'S EIGHTY-TWO — THE LONG YANG
   1. The Names and the Order of the Eighty-Two Forms
   2. Instructional Photographs
D. TAI CHI'S TWENTY-FOUR — THE SHORT YANG
   1. The Names and the Order of the Twenty-Four Forms

III. TAI CHI CHUAN'S SOLO EXERCISES

A. THE APPROACHES TO PRACTICE

Tai Chi's solo exercises vary in length from 24 to 250 movements, depending on the particular school of Tai Chi Chuan. No matter which solo exercise one practices, one should approach it according to the following procedures:

1. Know the general principles and rules of Tai Chi Chuan thoroughly.
2. In practice, first concentrate on the principles of balance and body mechanics. Second, stress the three principles of softness, slowness and flow of the 11 key points. Third, apply the principles of self-defense to the forms. Fourth, apply the principles and rules of breathing to these movements. Fifth, whenever practicing, concentrate your attention at all times on your three main centers: (a) your center of gravity, (b) your psychic-navel center and (c) the center in your mind.
3. Concentrate equally on the *technique of movement* and on the *technique of form.* The technique of movement is the coordination of the hands and feet within a form and the coordination of hands and feet between forms. The movement of the hands must finish simultaneously with the shift of weight from one foot to the other. The technique of form refers to the positions of the hands and feet at any point in a movement. For instance, the important position of the feet determines balance and direction of force. The position of the body determines balance and the efficiency of the force applied. The position of the arms and hands determines the efficiency of a punch or a block.
4. Master each section of Tai Chi's 82 before proceeding onto the next one. In other words, one should have mastered section one before proceeding onto section two.
5. Once one has learned the complete set, concentrate on finishing on the same spot as one begins.
6. Concentrate on taking as much time as possible to complete the set. The 82 movements should take at least 30 minutes when one has become proficient.
7. Learn to do the movements to the left as well as to the right.
8. Practice the solo sets at least twice a day.

9. If one has learned only the long form of the solo exercise and has little time available, one can practice any one of the three sections separately.
10. If one does a separate section of the long form to the left and to the right (left and right style), one will be able to begin and end on the same spot.
11. Do not forget that the principles of the Art of Joined Hands also apply in the solo exercise. To stick is to give complete attention to the forms and the movement from moment to moment. Not to resist is to be receptive and open so that one can let go and flow with the movements.
12. Whenever one practices the solo forms, one should remember to wait one-half hour after rising, one hour before eating, one hour after eating and one hour before going to bed.

B. PHILOSOPHICAL SIGNIFICANCE

One practices the movements of Tai Chi Chuan by moving from form to form without any break or change in tempo or rhythm. The many forms symbolize many living things. Continuous movement can be taken to mean that all life is in movement.

The beauty of Tai Chi Chuan does not lie in any particular form or movement, but in the action of the whole kaleidoscope of 82 movements from beginning to end; the beauty of life lies not in any one of its stages, but in the whole movement from birth to death.

C. TAI CHI'S EIGHTY-TWO — THE LONG YANG

1. THE NAMES AND THE ORDER OF THE EIGHTY-TWO FORMS

SECTION ONE

1. Beginning of Tai Chi
2. Grasp Bird's Tail Left
        Push Up, Pull Back, Press Forward and Push
3. Single Whip
4. Raise Hands and Step Up

5. White Stork Displays Its Wings
6. Brush Knee and Twist Left
7. Play Guitar
8. Brush Knee and Twist — Left, Right and Left
9. Play Guitar
10. Brush Knee and Twist Left
11. Deflect Sideways, Parry, Step Forward and Punch
12. Apparent Counter and Closure
13. Cross Hands

SECTION TWO

14. Carry Tiger Home To The Mountains
        Pull Back, Press Forward and Push
        Diagonal Single Whip
15. Fist Under Elbow
16. Fall Back and Twist Like Monkey
        — Right, Left, Right, Left, Right
17. Slanting Flying
18. Raise Hands and Step Up
19. White Stork Displays Its Wings
20. Brush Knee and Twist Left
21. Sea Bottom Needle
22. Fan Through The Back
23. Turn and Strike Opponent With Fist
24. Deflect Sideways, Parry, Step Forward and Punch
25. Grasp Bird's Tail, Step Up
        Push Up, Pull Back, Press Forward and Push
26. Single Whip
27. Wave Hands Like Clouds — Right and Left (5 Times)
28. Single Whip
29. High Pat On Horse
30. Separate Right and Left Foot
31. Turn and Kick With Sole
32. Brush Knee and Twist — Left and Right
33. Step Forward, Brush Knee and Punch Downward
34. Turn and Strike Opponent With Fist
35. Deflect Sideways, Parry, Step Up and Punch
36. Right Foot Kicks Up
37. Hit Tiger — Left and Right

38. Right Foot Kicks Up
39. Double Wind Blows Against Ears
40. Left Foot Kicks Up
41. Turn and Right Foot Kicks Up
42. Deflect Sideways, Parry, Step Up and Punch
43. Apparent Counter and Closure
44. Cross Hands

SECTION THREE

45. Carry Tiger Home To The Mountains
        Pull Back, Press Forward and Push
46. Horizontal Single Whip
47. Parting of Wild Horse's Mane — Right, Left, Right, Left, Right
48. Step Up, Grasp Bird's Tail Left
        Push Up, Pull Back, Press Forward and Push
49. Single Whip
50. Fair Lady Works At Shuttles
51. Step Up, Grasp Bird's Tail Left
        Push Up, Pull Back, Press Forward and Push
52. Single Whip
53. Wave Hands Like Clouds — Right and Left (Five Times)
54. Single Whip
        Snake Creeps Down
55. Golden Cock Stands On One Leg — Left and Right
56. Fall Back and Twist Like Monkey
        — Right, Left, Right, Left, Right
57. Slanting Flying
58. Raise Hands and Step Up
59. White Stork Displays Its Wings
60. Brush Knee and Twist Left
61. Sea Bottom Needle
62. Fan Through The Back
63. Turn and White Snake Spits Out Tongue
64. Deflect Sideways, Parry, Step Up and Punch
65. Grasp Bird's Tail, Step Up
        Push Up, Pull Back, Press Forward and Push
66. Single Whip
67. Wave Hands Like Clouds — Right and Left (Five Times)
68. Single Whip

69. High Pat On Horse
70. Five Darts Whistling Into The Cave
71. Turn and Cross Legs
72. Brush Knee and Punch Opponent's Pubic Region
73. Grasp Bird's Tail, Follow Up
        Push Up, Pull Back, Press Forward and Push
74. Single Whip
        Snake Creeps Down
75. Step Up To Form Seven Stars
76. Retreat To Ride The Tiger
77. Turn Around and Position The Lotus
78. Shoot Tiger With Drawn Bow
79. Deflect Sideways, Parry, Step Up and Punch
80. Apparent Counter and Closure
81. Cross Hands
82. End of Tai Chi

2. INSTRUCTIONAL PHOTOGRAPHS

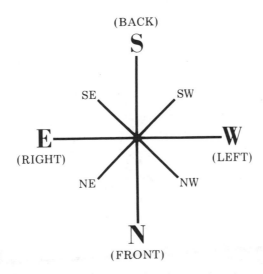

All directional instructions are given in relation to your position at the very beginning of the Long Yang. The direction you face originally is north; behind you is south; to your right is east; and to your left is west.

SECTION ONE:
1. THE BEGINNING OF TAI CHI

1a

(1a) Your eyes look straight ahead. Both arms hang straight down your sides, palms facing your thighs. Your feet are together and your toes point north. (1a-1) Your left foot steps a shoulder-width away from your right. Both palms turn south. (1a-2) Both arms rise to shoulder level, remaining a shoulder-width apart. Your palms face the floor and your fingers point north. (1a-3) Both arms fall gently to hang down the sides of your torso. Both palms remain facing the floor, fingers pointing north.

2. GRASP BIRD'S TAIL—LEFT, PUSH UP, PULL BACK, PRESS FORWARD AND PUSH

2a

2a. Grasp Bird's Tail—Left

(2a) Your right arm rises up to shoulder level, palm facing the floor, fingers pointing north. (2a-1) Both knees bend. (2a-2) Shift your weight to your left foot. (2a-3) Pivot lightly on your right heel until your foot faces directly east. At the same time, your torso turns to face east. Your eyes look east also. Your right arm forms a semi-circle with your right upper arm pointing directly east. Your right arm should be parallel to the floor, fingertips pointing northeast, palm facing down. (2a-4) Shift your weight to your right foot. At the same time, your left foot comes up on its ball and your left hand, palm facing upward, swings directly under your right hand. Your eyes look to the northeast. (2a-5) Your left foot, pointing directly northeast, steps to the northeast corner. (2a-6) Your weight shifts to your left foot. At the same time, your left arm, held in a half circle, rises up in a curve to shoulder level. Your left arm should now be parallel to the floor, your left palm facing your chest, your left wrist positioned over your center line. Your right hand, palm facing the floor, falls in a curve, coming to rest just in front of your right hip. Your right fingers and right toes both point east. For further visual clarification, see no. 83.

2a·4

2b. Push Up

(2b) Your eyes look east. Shift your weight to your left foot. Your right foot comes up on its ball. Your left palm turns downward. Your right hand, palm facing upward, swings directly under your left hand. (2b-1) Your right foot, pointing

1a·1

1a·2

1a·3

2a·1

2a·2

2a·3

2a·5

2a·6

2b

2b-1

directly east, steps to the east. (2b-2) Shift your weight to your right foot. Your right arm rises up to shoulder level. Your right arm should be parallel to the floor and form a semi-circle, palm facing your chest, wrist held over your center line. Your left elbow points downward. Your left palm, fingers pointing upward, even with your right elbow, faces your right wrist.

2c. Pull Back

(2c) Your right arm rises until your right wrist is at eye level. (2c-1) Your right hand swings across from left to right at eye level, moving until your right arm and hand are aligned with your right shoulder. At the same time, your left palm turns to face your right elbow. (2c-2) Simultaneously, your right palm turns downward and your left palm turns upward. (2c-3) Shift your weight to your left foot. Both hands and arms swing down, back, up and across to your left side. Your eyes look at your left hand.

2c-2

2d. Press Forward

(2d) Your right arm rises to a shoulder level position parallel to the floor, palm facing you. Turn your left palm upward. Bend your left elbow and swing your left palm over behind your right wrist. Your eyes look at your left palm. (2d-1) Shift your weight, evenly distributing it on both feet. Your left elbow should be down, your left fingers touching your right wrist. Your eyes look at your right wrist. (2d-2) Shift your weight to your right foot. Your hips turn until your torso faces east. Your right arm is held in a semi-circle parallel to the floor.

2e. Push

(2e) Your weight shifts to your left foot. Both hands spread a shoulder-width apart. Your palms turn to face east. Your elbows point down. Your eyes look east. (2e-1) Your weight shifts to your right foot. Both arms extend eastward. Your hands remain a shoulder-width apart at shoulder level. Your palms face forward, your fingers point upward.

2d-2

3. SINGLE WHIP

(3a) Shift your weight to your left foot. Both palms turn to face the floor. (3a-1) Turn your tor-

2b·2

2c

2c·1

2c·3

2d

2d·1

2e

2e·1

3a

so to the left as a complete unit, moving until you face northwest. Extend your arms and fingers to the northwest also. Your right heel pivots until your foot points northwest. Keep both knees bent. Your weight should be on your left foot, your eyes looking to the northwest. (3a-2) Your weight shifts to your right foot. Your torso turns until you face northeast, your arms and fingers extending to the northeast also. Your eyes look to the northeast. (3a-3) Your torso turns to face west. Your eyes look west. Your left foot, facing west, comes up on its ball one-half step in front of your right. Your right arm, bent slightly at the elbow, extends north to northeast. Your right wrist bends fully at eye level, fingertips pinched together and pointing to the floor. Your left arm, hand open, palm facing you, bends in a vertical curve, fingertips pointing upward at eye level. Your eyes look directly west. (3a-4) Your left palm turns to face west. (3a-5) Your left foot, pointing west, steps out. (3a-6) Your weight shifts to your left foot. Your left arm extends westward and your left palm, fingertips held at eye level, strikes out along your center line.

3a·1

3a·5

4. RAISE HANDS AND STEP UP
4a. Raise Hands
(4a) Your weight shifts to your right foot. Your torso turns to face north. Your left foot pivots on its heel until your foot points northwest. Your eyes look at your left hand. (4a-1) Your weight shifts to your left foot. Your eyes look directly north. Your right hand opens and both palms face inward. (4a-2) Raise your right leg until your thigh is parallel to the floor. Your right foot swings in and under your right thigh. Your left and right arms swing toward your center line. With your right shoulder leading, your right arm extends northward, fingertips held at eye level. Your left palm faces your right elbow. (4a-3) Your right foot steps down one-half step in front of your left and points north. Only your right heel touches the floor.

4b. Step Up
(4b) Your right leg rises up until your right thigh is again parallel to the floor. Your right foot swings in and under your right thigh. Your right arm falls down along your center line, coming to a rest next to your inner right knee and thigh and in front of your groin. Your left arm swings down, back and across on your left side, then extends behind you. (4b-1) Your right foot steps north one shoulder-width. It is placed parallel to your left foot and pointing northwest. Your weight shifts to your right foot. At the same time, your right hand and arm extend out just in front of your right knee. Your left palm turns upward, then your left arm bends. Your left hand rises up to your left ear and comes down to your chest, palm facing north. Your eyes look north.

4a·2

50

3a·2

3a·3

3a·4

3a·6

4a

4a·1

4a·3

4b

4b·1

5. WHITE STORK DISPLAYS ITS WINGS

5a

(5a) Your left foot moves one-half step to the west with only the ball of your foot touching the floor. Your weight remains on your right foot. Your hips turn your torso west. Your right arm, palm turning north, swings up to a shoulder level position parallel to the floor. Your left palm turns to angle westward but your left arm remains parallel to the floor. (5a-1) Your right arm rises up to eye level. Your left hand blocks downward and, moving from right to left, swings across your groin to a point near your left knee. Your left palm turns to face the floor, fingers pointing west. For further visual clarification, see no. 84.

6. BRUSH KNEE AND TWIST LEFT

6a-2

(6a) Your right elbow drops and points to the floor, palm turning to face you, fingers pointing to heaven. Your left palm turns toward your left thigh. (6a-1) As your right arm comes down and swings back, your left arm rises straight up to eye level along your left shoulder line. (6a-2) Then, it sweeps down and across to a shoulder level position parallel to the floor on your right shoulder line, palm facing down, fingers pointing northwest. Your right palm turns to face heaven. (6a-3) Your left foot, pointing directly west, steps forward. Your left palm sweeps down and forward, coming to a stop just outside your left thigh. With elbow bent, your right hand rises up near your right ear, palm facing west. (6a-4) Your weight shifts to your left foot. Your torso and eyes turn to face west. Your right palm strikes directly west along your center line, fingertips held at eye level. Your left arm extends downward, palm facing the floor, fingers pointing west, and comes to rest just in front of your left thigh.

7. PLAY GUITAR

7a-1

(7a) Raise your right foot just enough to clear the floor. (7a-1) Then, shift your weight to it and move it back to its position in no. 6a-4. (7a-2) Lift your left foot until your thigh is parallel to the floor. Tuck your left foot underneath your left thigh. Simultaneously, your left fingertips rise to eye level. Your right palm pulls back to face your left elbow. (7a-3) Your left heel comes down one-half step in front of your right foot. Your left hand comes down to shoulder level.

8. BRUSH KNEE AND TWIST—LEFT, RIGHT AND LEFT

8a. Brush Knee and Twist Left

(8a) Your torso turns to the right. At the same time, your left palm sweeps across to your right shoulder line and faces downward, fingertips pointing to the northwest. Your left arm is now parallel to the floor. Your right hand turns over and faces heaven at hip level. (8a-1) Your right

5a·1

6a

6a·1

6a·3

6a·4

7a

7a·2

7a·3

8a

arm sweeps straight back, palm turning to face heaven. (8a-2) Your left foot, pointing west, steps forward. Your left palm sweeps down and forward, coming to a stop just outside your left thigh. With elbow bent, your right hand rises up near your right ear, palm facing west. (8a-3) Your weight shifts to your left foot. Your right palm strikes directly westward along your center line, fingertips held at eye level. Your left hand extends downward on your left side, palm turning over to face the floor, fingers pointing forward, and comes to a rest just in front of your left thigh. Your eyes look west.

8b. Brush Knee and Twist Right

(8b) Your weight shifts to your right foot. At the same time, your left heel pivots until your left foot points southwest. Your left palm turns to face heaven. Your right palm sweeps across to your left shoulder line, then faces the floor, fingertips pointing southwest. Your torso turns to the left. (8b-1) Your weight shifts to your left foot. At the same time, your left hand swings back, palm facing heaven. (8b-2) Your right foot, pointing directly west, steps forward. Your right palm sweeps down, forward and to your right side, coming to a stop just outside your right thigh. Your left arm bends at the elbow and your left hand rises up alongside your left ear, palm facing forward. (8b-3) Your weight shifts to your right foot. At the same time, your left palm strikes directly westward along your center line, fingertips held at eye level. Your right arm moves over and your right hand comes to rest just in front of your right thigh, palm facing downward, fingers pointing forward. Your torso turns to the right to face directly west.

8c. Brush Knee and Twist Left

(8c) Your weight shifts to your left foot. Your right heel pivots until your right foot points directly northwest. Your torso turns to the right. Your right palm turns to face upward. Your left hand sweeps across to your right shoulder line, then faces downward, fingers pointing northwest. (8c-1) Your weight shifts to your right foot. At the same time, your right hand sweeps back and your right palm turns to face heaven. (8c-2) Your left foot, pointing directly west, steps forward. Your left palm sweeps down, forward and to your left side, coming to a stop just outside your left thigh. Your right arm bends at the elbow and your right hand rises up alongside your right ear, palm facing forward. (8c-3) Your weight shifts to your left foot. Your torso turns to the left and faces directly west. At the same time, your right palm strikes directly westward along your center line, fingertips held at eye level. Your left arm moves over and extends downward on your left side, palm facing the floor, fingers pointing forward. Your left hand comes to rest just in front of your left thigh. Your eyes look directly west.

8a·1

8b·1

8c·1

8a·2

8a·3

8b

8b·2

8b·3

8c

8c·2

8c·3

11a

9. PLAY GUITAR
Repeat nos. 7a to 7a-3 (not shown here).

10. BRUSH KNEE AND TWIST LEFT
Repeat nos. 8a to 8a-3 (not shown here).

11. DEFLECT SIDEWAYS, PARRY, STEP FORWARD AND PUNCH

11a. Deflect Sideways

11a·1

(11a) Shift to your right foot. Point your left foot southwest. Your torso turns to the left. Your left palm turns to face heaven. Your right hand sweeps across to your left shoulder line, then closes into a palm downward fist. (11a-1) Shift to your left foot. Your left arm swings and extends back, palm turning to face heaven. (11a-2) Your right foot moves forward on its heel one-half step in front of your left. (11a-3) Your torso turns to the right. Your right forearm, palm turning to face upward at shoulder level, sweeps across to your right shoulder line and forms an extended vertical "V". Your left hand rises up near your left ear.

11b. Parry

11c

(11b) Shift to your right foot. Your torso turns to the right. Your left palm strikes directly westward at eye level along your center line. Your right fist withdraws to your right side.

11c. Step Forward and Punch
(11c) Your left foot, pointing directly west, steps forward. Your torso turns to face northwest. Your left palm sweeps across to a position parallel to the floor on your right shoulder line, fingers pointing northwest, palm facing downward. (11c-1) Shift to your left foot. Your torso turns to face west. Your right fist, palm upward, strikes out along your center line, then turns south at chest level. Your left elbow hangs down, fingers pointing upward, palm facing your right forearm.

12. APPARENT COUNTER AND CLOSURE

12a. Apparent Counter

12a·2

(12a) Both palms turn to face heaven. Your left hand goes under and across your right upper arm. (12a-1) Shift to your right foot. As your right arm withdraws, your left wrist runs under and along it. (12a-2) Both hands spread a shoulder-width apart, palms facing west. Your elbows should be down and bent fully.

12b. Closure
(12b) Shift to your left foot. Both palms strike directly west at shoulder level.

13. CROSS HANDS
(13a) Your weight shifts to your right foot. Your torso turns to face directly north. Your arms form a circle, palms facing north, fingertips touching at eye level. Your left heel turns until your left foot points north. (13a-1) Your weight shifts to your

11a·2

11a·3

11b

11c·1

12a

12a·1

12b

13a

13a·1

left foot. Simultaneously, both palms circle downward on both sides. (13a-2) Both wrists cross at
abdomen level. (13a-3) Raise your right foot until
your thigh is parallel to the floor. Your arms form
a circle, palms facing you, wrists crossed at eye
level. Keep your wrists a good eight inches away
from your face. (13a-4) Your right foot steps
down a shoulder-width away from your left and
points directly north. Both knees bend. Your arms
drop until your wrists are at chest level, palms
facing you. Your eyes look directly north.

13a-2

SECTION TWO:

14. CARRY TIGER HOME TO THE MOUN-
TAINS, PULL BACK, PRESS FORWARD
AND PUSH, DIAGONAL SINGLE WHIP

14a. Carry Tiger Home to the Mountains
(14a) Shift your weight to your right foot. Keep
your right knee bent and pivot on your left heel
until your left foot points east. Your head turns
until your eyes look directly southeast. Your torso
faces east. At the same time, your right palm turns
to face downward and your left palm turns to face
upward. (14a-1) Shift your weight to your left
foot. At the same time, your right foot lifts up,
then comes down on its ball one-half step in front
of your left and pointing directly southeast. Your
left arm swings straight back, palm facing upward.
(14a-2) Your right foot, pointing southeast, steps
southeast. At the same time, your right hand
sweeps down from your left shoulder line to your
right shoulder line, stopping just in front of your
right knee. Your left arm bends at the elbow and
your left hand swings up alongside your left ear,
palm facing southeast. (14a-3) Your weight shifts
to your right foot. Your torso turns to face directly southeast. Your left palm strikes out along your
center line, fingertips held at eye level. Your right
palm turns to face downward just before and to
the side of your right thigh.

14a-1

14b. Pull Back
(14b) Your right hand rises up along your right
shoulder line to eye level, your palm turning to
face northeast. Your torso turns to the left and
your left arm drops slightly, your left palm turning
to face your right elbow. (14b-1) Your right palm
turns to face downward. At the same time, your
left palm turns to face upward. (14b-2) Your
weight shifts to your left foot. Both hands swing
down, up and back. Your eyes follow the movement of your hands. Your torso continues turning
to the left.

14b-1

14c. Press Forward
(14c) Your left arm bends at the elbow and your
left hand rises up to ear level, palm facing forward.
Your right arm rises up to shoulder level, palm
facing your chest. (14c-1) Your weight shifts until
it is equally distributed on both legs. Your left
fingertips touch the inside of your right wrist.
Your eyes look at your right wrist. (14c-2) Your

13a·3

13a·4

14a

14a·2

14a·3

14b

14b·2

14c

14c·1

14c·2

weight shifts to your right foot. Your torso faces southeast. Your right arm is held in a semi-circle, parallel to the floor at shoulder level. Your right fingers point to the northeast. Your eyes look to the southeast.

14d. Push

(14d) Your weight shifts to your left foot. As your arms pull back, both hands spread a shoulder-width apart and both palms turn to face southeast at shoulder level, fingers pointing upward. (14d-1) Your weight shifts to your right foot. Both hands strike out to the southeast. Your eyes look to the southeast.

14e. Diagonal Single Whip

(14e) Your weight shifts to your left foot. Both palms turn downward. (14e-1) Your torso turns to face directly north. Your eyes look north also. Both arms extend to the north. At the same time, your right heel turns until your right foot points north. Keep both knees bent. (14e-2) Your weight shifts to your right foot. At the same time, your torso turns to face northeast. Your eyes look to the northeast and your arms extend to the northeast. (14e-3) Your left leg rises until your left thigh is parallel to the floor and your left foot is tucked under your left thigh. Your torso turns to face northwest. Your eyes look to the northwest and your arms extend out to the northwest. (14e-4) Your left foot steps down, returning your left heel to its position in no. 14e-2. However, your left foot now points to the northwest. Your weight shifts to your left foot. (14e-5) Your right foot steps forward a shoulder-width, coming down so that the heels of both feet are aligned with each other in a north to south direction. Both feet point northwest. Your weight shifts to your right foot.

14e·1

15. FIST UNDER ELBOW

(15a) More weight shifts to your right foot. At the same time, your left knee bends and your left heel lifts off the floor. Your right arm bends and your right hand rises up to eye level, your right palm turning to face southwest. At the same time, your left hand lowers down to groin level. (15a-1) Your torso turns to the left until it faces directly west. Your eyes look west. Your left hand moves in close to your torso. (15a-2) Your right hand

14e·5

14d

14d·1

14e

14e·2

14e·3

14e·4

15a

15a·1

15a·2

sweeps across to your left shoulder line at chest level, palm facing downward. Your left hand rises before you, palm facing west, fingers pointing up. Hold your left thigh parallel to the floor, your left foot tucked beneath it. (15a-3) Toes pointing west, your left heel comes down one-half step in front of your right. Your left palm strikes westward at eye level along your center line. Bring your right fist, palm facing east, under your left elbow.

15a·3

16. FALL BACK AND TWIST LIKE MONKEY—RIGHT, LEFT, RIGHT, LEFT, RIGHT

16a. Twisting Monkey—Right

(16a) Your left palm turns toward heaven. Your open right hand lowers down on your right side. (16a-1) Your left foot steps back on its ball so your weight is evenly distributed. Your torso turns to the right. Your right hand swings back until both arms, palms upward, are aligned at shoulder level. (16a-2) Your left heel comes down, toes pointing southwest. Shift to your left foot. Bend your left knee. Your right hand, palm facing forward, swings up near your right ear. (16a-3) Your torso turns to the left. Point your right foot west. Your right palm strikes westward at eye level along your center line. Your left hand, palm facing upward, withdraws to your left side. Your eyes look west.

16a·3

16b. Twisting Monkey—Left

(16b) Your right foot steps back on its ball so your weight is evenly distributed. Swing your left hand back and align it with your right. Both palms face upward. (16b-1) Shift to your right foot. Your right heel comes down, toes pointing northwest. Your left hand rises up near your left ear, palm facing forward. (16b-2) Your torso turns to the right. Point your left foot west. Your left palm strikes westward at eye level along your center line. Your right hand, palm upward, withdraws to your right side.

16c. Twisting Monkey—Right, Left, Right

(16c) Your right hand swings back in line with your left at shoulder level. Both palms face upward. Your left foot steps back on its ball so your weight is evenly distributed. To complete this form, continue by repeating nos. 16a-2 to 16c, then 16a-2 and 16a-3.

16c

17. SLANTING FLYING

(17a) Your right foot steps back on its ball. Your right palm sweeps across and turns downward on your left shoulder line. Your left hand moves directly under it. (17a-1) Your weight shifts to your right foot, toes pointing northwest. Point your left foot north. Bend your right knee. Both hands circle clockwise until your left palm is on top facing downward and your right palm is below facing upward (like turning a car wheel). (17a-2) Shift to your left foot. (17a-3) Your head

16a

16a·1

16a·2

16b

16b·1

16b·2

17a

17a·1

17a·2

turns northeast. Your torso turns to the right. Your right foot comes up on its ball one-half step in front of your left and (17a-4) moves northeast. (17a-5) Shift to your right foot. Your right palm, facing upward, rises to eye level along your left shoulder line, then crosses over to your right shoulder line. Bring your left hand, palm facing downward, fingers pointing north, near your left thigh.

17a-3

18. RAISE HANDS AND STEP UP
18a. Raise Hands
(18a) Raise your left foot. (18a-1) Your head and torso turn north. Your left foot, now pointing northwest, steps down.
18b. Step Up
Repeat nos. 4a-2 to 4b-1 (not shown here).

19. WHITE STORK DISPLAYS ITS WINGS
Repeat nos. 5a to 5a-1 (not shown here).

20. BRUSH KNEE AND TWIST LEFT
Repeat nos. 6a to 7a (not shown here).

21. SEA BOTTOM NEEDLE
(21a) Your right foot, pointing northwest, steps down and carries your weight. Begin moving your right hand toward your right ear. Your left hand, palm facing downward, begins to strike out at solar plexus level. (21a-1) Hold your left thigh parallel to the floor, your left foot tucked under it. Follow-through with your hand movements. (21a-2) Your left foot, pointing west, steps down on its ball. Bend both knees and lean forward. Keep your head up. Your right hand, palm facing south, strikes down near your inner left knee. Your left hand, palm facing downward, fingers pointing forward, moves outside your left knee. Your eyes look west.

18a-1

22. FAN THROUGH THE BACK
(22a) Straighten up. Your open left hand rises up to throat level, palm facing west. Your right arm rises up to a face level position parallel to the floor, palm facing northwest. (22a-1) Your left foot steps to the west. Shift your weight to it. Your left palm strikes westward at eye level along your center line. Your right arm rises to eye level, palm facing north.

22a

23. TURN AND STRIKE OPPONENT WITH FIST
(23a) Shift to your right foot. Your torso turns north; your head, east. Point your left foot northeast. Hold your left forearm 45 degrees to the floor, palm facing north, and form a "V". Hold your right arm, fist closed, palm downward, across your waist and parallel to the floor. (23a-1) Shift to your left foot. Your torso faces northeast. Hold your right thigh parallel to the floor, your right foot tucked beneath it. Your right foot faces east.

17a·4

17a·5

18a

21a

21a·1

21a·2

22a·1

23a

23a·1

23a·2

(23a-2) Your right foot, pointing east, steps down. (23a-3) Your weight shifts to your right foot. Your right fist, knuckles leading, strikes overhead in a clockwise movement, traveling down your center line and coming to a stop at eye level, palm facing upward. Your left palm strikes backward in a counterclockwise movement. Your left arm extends backward, palm downward and fingers pointing west. (23a-4) Your left palm turns to face heaven. (23a-5) Your left hand swings down and up in a counterclockwise movement, like a left uppercup, palm facing east, fingers pointing to heaven, fingertips held at eye level. Your right fist withdraws to the right side of your waist, palm facing upward.

24. DEFLECT SIDEWAYS, PARRY, STEP FORWARD AND PUNCH
24a. Deflect Sideways

(24a) Your right fist opens. Your weight shifts to your left foot. Your left hand lowers. Your right palm sweeps upward from your right shoulder line and across to your center line at eye level. Your right palm faces north. (24a-1) Your right palm sweeps across to your left shoulder line, turns to face downward and closes into a fist at shoulder level. Your right arm is held in a semi-circle in front of your chest and is parallel to the floor. Your left hand, palm facing upward, withdraws to the front of your left hip. (24a-2) Your right leg rises upward until your right thigh is parallel to the floor and your right foot is tucked under your right thigh. Your left hand, palm facing north, sweeps back. (24a-3) Your right heel comes down one-half step in front of your left foot. (24a-4) Your right elbow drops and your right palm turns to face upward. Your right arm is bent with your right fist held at shoulder level. The outside of your right forearm sweeps across to your right shoulder line. Your left hand, palm facing forward, sweeps up alongside your left ear.

24a

24b. Parry

(24b) Your weight shifts to your right foot. Your right foot points southeast. Your left palm strikes eastward along your center line, fingertips held at eye level. Your right fist withdraws to. the right side of your waist, palm facing upward. Your eyes look east.

24c. Step Forward and Punch

(24c) Your left foot, pointing east, steps forward. Your left palm sweeps across to your right shoulder line, then turns to face downward. (24c-1) Your weight shifts to your left foot. Your right fist strikes eastward along your center line at sternum level. At the last moment of your arm's extension, your right palm moves from an upward position to one facing north. Your left elbow drops and your left palm, fingers pointing upward, faces your inner right arm.

24a·4

23a·3

23a·4

23a·5

24a·1

24a·2

24a·3

24b

24c

24c·1

25a

25. GRASP BIRD'S TAIL, STEP FORWARD, PUSH UP, PULL BACK, PRESS FORWARD AND PUSH

25a. Grasp Bird's Tail

(25a) Shift to your right foot. Your open right hand withdraws to your right side. Your left palm sweeps across to your right shoulder line, then faces down. (25a-1) Point your left foot northeast. Your left hand, palm facing east, sweeps across your face and, (25a-2) traveling in a counterclockwise circle, moves down your left shoulder line. Your right hand begins moving in a counterclockwise circle and sweeps across to a face level position even with your center line. (25a-3) Your left palm turns upward. Your right palm sweeps across to your left shoulder line and turns downward. (25a-4) Half your weight shifts to your left foot. Your right hand, outer edge leading, strikes forward and down. Your left hand withdraws and rises up to chest level. (25a-5) Shift to your left foot. Your left hand strikes out at throat level, palm facing downward. Your right palm turns upward under your left. In nos. 25a to 25a-3, visualize yourself turning a steering wheel counterclockwise. In nos. 25a-4 to 25a-5, visualize yourself turning a bicycle wheel forward.

25a·4

25b. Step Forward and Push Up

(25b) Your right foot steps forward. (25b-1) Then, repeat no. 2b-2 (not shown here).

25c. Pull Back

Repeat nos. 2c to 2c-3 (not shown here).

25d. Press Forward

Repeat nos. 2d to 2d-2 (not shown here).

25e. Push

Repeat nos. 2e to 2e-1 (not shown here).

26. SINGLE WHIP

Repeat nos. 3a to 3a-6 (not shown here).

27. WAVE HANDS LIKE CLOUDS—RIGHT AND LEFT (FIVE TIMES)

27a. Wave Hands Like Clouds

27a·1

(27a) Shift to your right foot. Point your left foot north. Your torso faces northeast. Your head turns toward your right hand which opens, palm facing downward. Your left hand swings down under your right. (27a-1) Your weight shifts evenly over both feet. Your left hand rises to eye level and your right lowers to abdomen level. Both palms face you and are in line with each other, one above, the other below. (27a-2) Your torso faces north. Your arms should form half circles and, throughout this set of movements, be opposite to and in line with each other. (27a-3) Shift to your left foot. Your head and torso turn west. (27a-4) Your left palm turns downward.

25a·1

25a·2

25a·3

25a·5

25b

27a

27a·2

27a·3

27a·4

27b

27b. Cloud Hands-Right

(27b) As your left hand drops down, your right hand rises up until your right palm faces your eyes. At the same time, your right foot steps inward to a position parallel to and about one-half shoulder-width to one fist distance away from your left foot. (27b-1) Your head and torso turn as one unit to face directly north. Your arms move with your torso. Your weight is now evenly distributed on both feet. (27b-2) Your weight shifts to your right foot. Your head and torso turn to face directly east. Your feet remain pointing north. Your arms and hands move with your torso. (27b-3) Your right palm turns downward.

27c. Cloud Hands—Left

(27c) Pointing north, your left foot steps directly west. Your left hand rises up until your left palm faces your eyes. Your right palm lowers down to abdomen level. (27c-1) Your weight shifts until it is evenly distributed on both feet. Your head and torso turn to face north. Your arms and hands move with your torso. (27c-2) Your weight shifts to your left foot. Your head and torso turn to face west. Your arms and hands move with your torso. (27c-3) Your left palm turns downward. Repeat nos. 27b to 27c-3 four additional times. Each step out with your left foot counts as one completed sequence. When you have stepped out with your left foot five times, you will have executed the Wave Hands with Clouds form, right and left, the required five times.

27c

28. SINGLE WHIP

(28a) Pointing northwest, your right foot moves one-half step toward your left. At the same time, your right hand rises up until its palm faces your eyes. Your left hand lowers downward to abdomen level. (28a-1) Your right hand continues in a clockwise circle, rising above your eyes. Your torso continues turning to the right. Your left hand sweeps down and in toward your abdomen. (28a-2) Your right hand, fingers pinched together, continues in a clockwise circle. Your right arm extends out to the northeast. Your left hand rises up to chest level. Then, repeat nos. 3a-3 to 3a-6 as shown earlier (not pictured here).

28a

29. HIGH PAT ON HORSE

(29a) Your left palm turns upward. Your right hand opens, palm facing downward, and moves next to your right ear. (29a-1) Shift your weight

27b·1

27b·2

27b·3

27c·1

27c·2

27c·3

28a·1

28a·2

29a

to your right foot. As your left foot draws back one-half step, it comes up on its ball and rests lightly on the floor, toes pointing straight west. Simultaneously, your left hand, palm facing upward, draws back to rest alongside your waist. At the same time, the outer edge of your right palm strikes out at throat level.

30. SEPARATE RIGHT AND LEFT FOOT
30a. Separate Right Foot

(30a) With your hands and arms remaining in their previous position, your left foot steps out to the southwest corner. Your weight shifts to it. Your right arm extends out, palm facing downward. Your left arm, palm facing upward, extends out directly under your right. Your eyes remain looking west. (30a-1) Your weight remains on your left foot. Pivoting on your waist and hips, turn until you face north. Do not move your arms or hands. They will move with your torso as it pivots on your hips. (30a-2) Turn back until you again face west. Your right hand sweeps down to groin level in a circular motion. At the same time, your left hand rises up until its palm faces your right shoulder. Your body weight should still be on your left foot. (30a-3) Your right arm rises and your right wrist crosses over your left wrist at chest level. At the same time, your right foot rises up until your right thigh is parallel to the floor, your right heel tucked under your right thigh. Simultaneously, your eyes and your right shoulder turn until they face northwest. (30a-4) Your right and left arms extend out on a horizontal plane, opening up like a flower bud blooming. Both left and right fingertips should be at eye level and pointing to heaven. Your right foot kicks out in a curve, moving from west to northwest, and makes contact with the toes. Your right thigh should remain parallel to the floor. Your right arm and leg should be in line with each other and both should be extending to the northwest.

30b. Separate Left Foot

(30b) Your right foot draws back into its position in no. 30a-3. Your arms and hands remain extended. (30b-1) Your right foot steps down toward the northwest corner. (30b-2) As your weight shifts to your right foot, your right hand descends to hip level, palm facing upward. Your left hand sweeps across at shoulder level and ends, palm facing downward, directly above your right hand. Your eyes turn to face west. (30b-3 to 30b-6) The movements here are identical to those in nos. 30a-1 to 30a-4. In 30a-1 to 30a-4, however, you began with your right hand on top and kicked with your right foot, while here you begin with your left hand on

30a

30a·1

30a·2

30a·4

30b

30b·1

30b·3

30b·4

30b·5

top and kick with your left foot. You also face southwest instead of northwest as in the no. 30a sequence.

30b-6

31. TURN AND KICK WITH SOLE

(31a) Your left foot draws back to its position in no. 30b-5. (31a-1) Pivoting on your right foot, face east. Point your right foot southeast. Cross both wrists at chest level. Turn your left shoulder eastward. Your eyes should be looking east also. (31a-2) As your left heel again kicks out, both arms form semi-circles and extend outward horizontally, opening up like a flower bud blooming in the spring. Point your fingertips to heaven at eye level.

32. BRUSH KNEE AND TWIST—LEFT AND RIGHT

32a. Brush Knee and Twist Left

(32a) Withdraw your left foot and tuck it under your left thigh. Your left arm remains extended, palm facing downward, forearm parallel to the floor, fingertips pointing southeast. Your right arm extends straight back, palm facing upward. (32a-1) Your left foot steps down, toes pointing east. Your left palm sweeps down toward your left thigh. Elbow bent, your right hand, palm angled forward, rises up near your right ear. (32a-2) Shift to your left foot. Your right palm strikes directly eastward at eye level along your center line. Your left hand rests in front of your left thigh, palm facing the floor, fingers pointing forward.

32a

32b. Brush Knee and Twist Right

(32b) Your weight shifts to your right foot. Your right palm sweeps across to your left shoulder line, then turns down at shoulder level. Your left palm turns to face upward. Your left heel pivots until your foot points northeast. Your eyes look east. (32b-1) Your weight shifts to your left foot. Your left hand sweeps back, palm facing upward. (32b-2) Your right foot, pointing east, steps east. Your right hand sweeps down from your left shoulder line to your right shoulder line, ending just in front of your right thigh, palm facing south. Your left hand sweeps up alongside your left ear, palm facing forward. (32b-3) Your weight shifts to your right foot. Your left palm strikes eastward along your center line, fingertips held at eye level. Your right palm turns to face down and withdraws to just in front of and alongside your right thigh.

32b-1

33. STEP FORWARD, BRUSH KNEE AND PUNCH DOWNWARD

33a. Step Forward and Brush Knee

(33a) Your weight shifts to your left foot. Your right foot pivots until it faces southeast. Your left hand sweeps across to your right shoulder line and your palm turns to face the floor at shoulder level. Your right hand rises to waist level and closes into

31a

31a·1

31a·2

32a·1

32a·2

32b

32b·2

32b·3

33a

33a·1

a fist, palm facing upward. (33a-1) Your left foot, pointing east, steps forward. Your left hand sweeps down from your right shoulder line to your left shoulder line, ending just in front of your left thigh, palm facing north.

33b. Punch Downward

(33b) Your weight shifts to your left foot. Your right fist punches down along your center line, your palm turning to face north at the last moment.

34a·2

34. TURN AND STRIKE OPPONENT WITH FIST

(34a to 34a-6) The movements here are identical to those in nos. 23a to 23a-5. The only differences are: 1) you turn to face west instead of east, and 2) unlike the earlier movements where your torso faced east at a half slant as you turned around, your torso now faces directly west.

35. DEFLECT SIDEWAYS, PARRY, STEP UP AND PUNCH

35a. Deflect Sideways

(35a to 35a-3) The movements here are identical to those in nos. 23a-5 to 24a-2. However, you are facing west now instead of east. Continue by following these movements with those of nos. 11a-2 and 11a-3 as shown earlier (not pictured here).

34a·6

33b

34a

34a·1

34a·3

34a·4

34a·5

35a

35a·1

35a·2

35b. Parry
Repeat the movements of no. 11b as shown earlier (not pictured here).
35c. Step Up and Punch
Repeat the movements of nos. 11c to 11c-1 as shown earlier (not pictured here).

36. RIGHT FOOT KICKS UP
(36a) Your weight shifts to your right foot. Your left heel pivots until your foot points southwest. Your eyes look west. Both arms form a wedge which points southwest at eye level, your palms facing out, fingertips touching. (36a-1) Your weight shifts to your left foot. Both hands draw a circle, sweeping out and down on both sides of your torso. (36a-2) Both hands rise up in front of your chest and cross at the wrists, palms facing your torso. Your torso faces southwest. Your right leg rises up until your right thigh is parallel to the floor and your right foot is tucked under your right thigh. (36a-3) Your right foot kicks directly westward. Your hands open out on a horizontal plane, like a flower blossoming in the spring. Your right arm and leg are in alignment. Both palms face outward and are on the same level. Your eyes look directly west.

37. HIT TIGER—LEFT AND RIGHT
37a. Hit Tiger Left
(37a) Your right foot withdraws under your right thigh. (37a-1) Your right foot steps down next to your left. Both feet point to the southwest. Both hands come together in front of your chest, closing into fists, palms facing southwest, at shoulder level. Your torso faces southwest. Your eyes look at both fists. (37a-2) Your left foot, pointing south, steps back to the northeast. Both fists drop down to hip level. (37a-3) Your weight shifts to your left foot. Your left fist swings back and up in a clockwise circle, ending in front of your forehead, palm facing south. Your left forearm should be held at a 30 to 45-degree angle to the floor. Your right hand swings down and up in a clockwise movement, your right forearm ending parallel to the floor at waist level and your right fist, palm facing downward, ending in front and to the left of your torso. Your eyes look directly west.

37b. Hit Tiger Right
(37b) Your right foot lifts up. (37b-1) Your right foot steps to the west. Your left fist swings overhead and back in a counterclockwise movement. (37b-2 to 37b-3) Your weight shifts to your right foot. Your torso turns to the right and faces west. Your right fist swings up and over in a counterclockwise movement, ending in front of your forehead, palm facing west. Your right forearm should be at a 30 to 45-degree angle to the floor. Your left fist continues its counterclockwise movement and ends just in front and to the right of your torso, palm facing downward, forearm parallel to

35a·3

36a·3

37a·3

36a

36a·1

36a·2

37a

37a·1

37a·2

37b

37b·1

37b·2

37b·3

the floor at waist level. Your eyes look directly west. For further visual clarification of these movements, see nos. 85a to 85b-3.

38. RIGHT FOOT KICKS UP
(38a) Your weight shifts to your left foot. Both fists open and rise to eye level. Your torso turns to the left and faces southwest. Your arms form a wedge to the southwest, palms facing outward. (38a-1) Both palms draw a circle, sweeping out and down on both sides of your torso. (38a-2 to 38a-3) Repeat the movements of nos. 36a-2 and 36a-3 as explained earlier.

38a·3

39. DOUBLE WIND BLOWS AGAINST EARS
(39a) Repeat the movement of no. 37a as explained earlier. (39a-1) Your left heel pivots until your foot points west. Both arms move in and extend to the northwest, palms facing upward, fingertips held at shoulder level. Your torso turns to face northwest and your eyes look northwest also. (39a-2) Your right foot, pointing northwest, steps to the northwest. Both hands fall down along your center line, then split out to your sides at hip level. (39a-3) Your weight shifts to your right foot. Both hands close into fists and rise up in half circles, meeting at ear level, index knuckles leading, palms facing the floor. Be sure that your arms form a large circle. Your eyes look northwest.

40. LEFT FOOT KICKS UP
(40a) Your weight shifts to your left foot. Both fists open. (40a-1) Your weight shifts to your right foot. At the same time, both hands circle out and down on both sides. Your head turns and your eyes look west. (40a-2) Both hands rise inward and up in front of your chest, crossing at the wrists. Your left leg rises up until your left thigh is parallel to the floor and your left foot is tucked under your left thigh. Your torso remains facing north-

39a·3

38a

38a·1

38a·2

39a

39a·1

39a·2

40a

40a·1

40a·2

west. (40a-3) Your left foot kicks westward. Your hands, palms facing outward, spread horizontally at eye level. Align your left arm and leg.

40a·3

41. TURN AND RIGHT FOOT KICKS UP
(41a) Your left foot sweeps down and back. (41a-1 to 41a-3) Pivoting on the ball of your right foot, kick your left out and around in a 360-degree clockwise sweep. Bring it down, pointing southwest, one-half step behind your right. Your arms move with the pivot. Your torso faces southwest; your eyes, west. (41a-4) Shift to your left foot. Your right foot, pointing west, comes up on its ball. Your wrists cross over your chest. (41a-5) Repeat no. 36a-2. Then, repeat no. 36a-3 (not shown here).

42. DEFLECT SIDEWAYS, PARRY, STEP UP AND PUNCH
42a. Deflect Sideways
(42a) Your right hand closes into a fist. Tuck your right foot under your right thigh. Now, repeat no. 11a-3 (not shown here).
42b. Parry
Repeat no. 11b (not shown here).
42c. Step Up and Punch
Repeat nos. 11c and 11c-1 (not shown here).

41a·3

43. APPARENT COUNTER AND CLOSURE
Repeat nos. 12a to 12b (not shown here).

44. CROSS HANDS
Repeat nos. 13a to 13a-4 (not shown here).

SECTION THREE:
45. CARRY TIGER HOME TO THE MOUNTAINS, PULL BACK, PRESS FORWARD AND PUSH
Repeat nos. 14a to 14d-1 (not shown here).

46. HORIZONTAL SINGLE WHIP
(46a to 46a-2) Repeat nos. 14e to 14e-2 (not shown here). (46a-3) Your torso turns north; your eyes, northwest. Your left foot, pointing northwest, comes up on its ball one-half step in front of your right. Your right arm extends east/northeast, fingertips pinched together pointing downward at eye level. Your left arm curves upward, palm facing you, fingertips pointing upward at eye level. (46a-4) Your left foot steps northwest. Your left palm turns northwest. (46a-5) Shift to your left foot. Your left palm strikes to the northwest at eye level along your center line.

46a·3

47. PARTING OF WILD HORSE'S MANE— RIGHT, LEFT, RIGHT, LEFT, RIGHT
47a. Parting Right
(47a) Shift to your right foot. Your head and torso turn east. Point your left foot northeast. Your arms turn with your torso. (47a-1) Your right foot

41a

41a·1

41a·2

41a·4

41a·5

42a

46a·4

46a·5

47a

83

comes up on its ball one-half step in front of your left. Your left palm turns downward on your left shoulder line. Your right palm, facing upward, moves directly under it. (47a-2) Your right foot, pointing east, steps east and (47a-3) carries your weight. Your right hand, describing a clockwise quarter circle, rises to eye level on your left shoulder line, then moves to extend just outside your right shoulder line, palm facing upward. Your left palm, facing downward, fingers pointing northeast, lowers toward your outer left thigh.

47b. Parting Left

(47b) Shift to your left foot. Your right hand sweeps across to shoulder level on your left shoulder line, palm facing downward, forearm pointing northeast. Your eyes look east. (47b-1) Point your right foot southeast and shift to it. As your torso turns southeast, your right forearm points east. Your left hand, palm facing upward, sweeps under your right. (47b-2) Your left foot, pointing east, steps forward and (47b-3) carries your weight. Your left hand, describing a counterclockwise quarter circle, rises to eye level on your right shoulder line, then moves to extend just outside your left shoulder line, palm facing upward. Your right palm, facing downward, fingers pointing southeast, lowers toward your outer right thigh.

47c. Parting Right, Left, Right

(47c) Shift to your right foot. Your left hand sweeps across to shoulder level on your right shoulder line, palm facing downward, forearm pointing southeast. Your eyes look east. (47c-1) Point your left foot northeast and shift to it. As your torso turns to face northeast, your left forearm points east. Your right hand, palm facing upward, sweeps under your left. To complete this form, repeat nos. 47a-2 to 47c-1, then 47a-2 again and 47a-3.

48. GRASP BIRD'S TAIL—LEFT, PUSH UP, PULL BACK, PRESS FORWARD AND PUSH

(48a) Your left foot comes up on its ball. Your right palm turns downward at shoulder level. Your left palm, facing upward, sweeps under your right. Now, repeat nos. 2a-5 to 2e-1 (not shown here).

49. SINGLE WHIP

Repeat nos. 3a to 3a-6 (not shown here).

50. FAIR LADY WORKS AT SHUTTLES #1, #2, #3 and #4

50a. #1

(50a) Shift to your right foot. Your head and torso turn northeast. Point your left foot north. Your arms move with your torso. (50a-1) Shift to your left foot. Point your right foot northeast. Elbow bent, your right hand comes to your center line, fingers pinched together pointing downward. Your left palm sweeps under and faces your right elbow.

47a·2

47a·3

47b

47b·2

47b·3

47c

48a

50a

50a·1

(50a-2) Your right heel comes down on the spot previously occupied by the ball of your foot. Point your right foot east and shift your weight to it. (50a-3) Your left foot, pointing east/northeast, steps to the northeast. Your right hand opens, palm facing downward. (50a-4) Shift to your left foot. Your torso turns northeast. Your right palm strikes to the northeast at eye level along your center line. Your left arm rolls up in a clockwise circle, ending with your forearm 30 to 45 degrees to the floor, your palm facing outward just above your forehead. Your eyes look northeast.

50a·2

50b. #2

(50b) Your left arm and hand, palm facing downward, lower to shoulder level. Your right hand lowers down to waist level, facing upward directly under your left. (50b-1) Your weight shifts to your right foot. Your head and torso turn as far to the right as is physically possible. Your arms and hands move with the turning of your torso. Your left foot pivots as far to the right as possible. (50b-2) Your weight shifts to your left foot. Your right foot steps directly northwest and is placed so that it points west to northwest. Your head and eyes turn to face northwest. (50b-3) Your weight shifts to your right foot. Your left heel pivots until your foot points west. Your left palm strikes to the northwest along your center line, fingertips held at eye level. Your right arm and hand roll up before you in a counterclockwise circle, ending with your right forearm in a 30 to 45-degree angle to the floor and your palm facing outward just above your forehead. Your eyes look directly northwest.

50b·1

50c. #3

(50c) Your left hand turns to face downward at shoulder level. Your right arm lowers to chest level, palm facing downward behind your left forearm. Your right fingers point southwest. Your head turns to face southwest. Your left foot lifts its heel and comes up on its ball. (50c-1) Your left foot, pointing west, steps directly southwest. (50c-2) Your weight shifts to your left foot. Your right heel turns until your foot points west. Your right palm strikes to the southwest along your center line, fingertips held at eye level. Your left hand and arm roll up before you in a clockwise circle, ending with your left forearm in a 30 to 45-degree angle to the floor, palm facing outward just above your forehead. Your eyes look directly southwest.

50c·1

50d. #4

(50d) Your left hand and arm lower to shoulder level, palm facing downward. Your right hand, palm up, lowers to a waist-level position directly under your left hand. (50d-1) Your weight shifts to your right foot. Your head and torso turn to the right as far as is physically possible. Your arms and hands move with your torso. Your left heel

50a·3

50a·4

50b

50b·2

50b·3

50c

50c·2

50d

50d·1

pivots as far right as possible. (50d-2) Shift to your left foot. Your right foot, pointing east/southeast, steps southeast. (50d-3) Shift to your right foot. Your head and torso face southeast. Point your left foot east. Your left palm strikes southeast at eye level on your center line. Your right arm rolls up in a counterclockwise circle, forearm 30 to 45 degrees to the floor, palm facing outward just above your forehead.

50d·2

51. STEP UP, GRASP BIRD'S TAIL—LEFT, PUSH UP, PULL BACK, PRESS FORWARD AND PUSH

Repeat nos. 48a, 2a-5 to 2e-1 (not shown here).

52. SINGLE WHIP

Repeat nos. 3a to 3a-6 (not shown here).

53. WAVE HANDS LIKE CLOUDS—RIGHT AND LEFT (FIVE TIMES)

Repeat nos. 27a to 27c-3 (not shown here).

54. SINGLE WHIP, SNAKE CREEPS DOWN

54a. Single Whip

Repeat nos. 28a to 28a-2, 3a-3 to 3a-6 (not shown here).

54b·2

54b. Snake Creeps Down

(54b) Your left palm faces heaven. Point your right foot northeast. (54b-1) As your right knee bends, shift to your right foot. Your left hand draws back, elbow sliding behind your left side. (54b-2) Fingers pointing downward, the back of your left hand slides along the left side of your torso, past your left thigh to your left knee. (54b-3) Your right knee bends deeper and your left hand slides down to your left foot. Bend your left knee only slightly.

55. GOLDEN COCK STANDS ON ONE LEG —LEFT AND RIGHT

55a. Left Stance

(55a) Point your left foot southwest and shift your weight to it. Your left palm rises, extends west and (55a-1) faces the floor. Point your right foot northwest. Your right hand opens, swinging toward your right hip, palm facing downward, fingers pointing forward. (55a-2) Your left hand swings toward your left hip, palm facing downward, fingers pointing southwest. Both your right hand and knee rise. Your right arm extends along your center line, palm facing west at eye level. Hold your right thigh parallel to the floor, your lower right leg hanging, relaxed.

55a·2

55b. Right Stance

(55b) Your right foot, pointing northwest, steps back and (55b-1) carries your weight. (55b-2) Your right hand moves down on your right side. Your left palm faces west at eye level. Hold your left thigh parallel to the floor, your lower leg hanging, relaxed.

50d·3

54b

54b·1

54b·3

55a

55a·1

55b

55b·1

55b·2

60a

56. FALL BACK AND TWIST LIKE MONKEY—RIGHT, LEFT, RIGHT, LEFT, RIGHT

Repeat nos. 16a-1 to 16c, 16a-2 to 16c again, ending with 16a-2 and 16a-3 (not shown here).

57. SLANTING FLYING

Repeat nos. 17a to 17a-5 (not shown here).

58. RAISE HANDS AND STEP UP

Repeat nos. 18a and 18a-1, 4a-2 to 4b-1 (not shown here).

59. WHITE STORK DISPLAYS ITS WINGS

Repeat nos. 5a to 5a-1 (not shown here).

60. BRUSH KNEE AND TWIST LEFT

(60a to 60a-5) Repeat nos. 6a to 7a.

61. SEA BOTTOM NEEDLE

(61a to 61a-2) Repeat nos. 21a to 21a-2.

60a·4

62. FAN THROUGH THE BACK

(62a to 62a-1) Repeat nos. 22a to 22a-1.

63. TURN AND WHITE SNAKE SPITS OUT TONGUE

(63a to 63a-2) Repeat nos. 23a to 23a-2 (not shown here). (63a-3 to 63a-5) Move as in nos. 23a-3 to 23a-5 but keep your right hand open throughout and turn your left palm west as it swings backward.

64. DEFLECT SIDEWAYS, PARRY, STEP UP AND PUNCH

Repeat nos. 24a to 24c-1 (not shown here).

65. GRASP BIRD'S TAIL, STEP UP, PUSH UP, PULL BACK, PRESS FORWARD AND PUSH

Repeat nos. 25a to 25b, 2b-2 to 2e-1 (not shown here).

61a·2

66. SINGLE WHIP

Repeat nos. 3a to 3a-6 (not shown here).

67. WAVE HANDS LIKE CLOUDS—RIGHT AND LEFT (FIVE TIMES)

Repeat nos. 27a to 27c-3 (not shown here).

68. SINGLE WHIP

Repeat nos. 28a to 28a-2, 3a-3 to 3a-6 (not shown here).

69. HIGH PAT ON HORSE

Repeat nos. 29a to 29a-1 (not shown here).

60a·1

60a·2

60a·3

60a·5

61a

61a·1

62a

62a·1

63a·3

70. FIVE DARTS WHISTLING INTO THE CAVE

(70a) Your right arm lowers to waist level. (70a-1) Your left foot, pointing west, steps west and carries your weight. Your left fingertips, palm up, strike west at throat level. Your right palm, facing downward, ends below your left elbow. Your eyes look west.

71. TURN AND CROSS LEGS

(71a) Shift to your right foot. Your head turns east. Your right forearm, fist clenched, is at waist level and parallel to the floor. Your left palm, facing north, swings over above your head, forearm held 30 to 45 degrees to the floor. Bend both knees. (71a-1) Shift to your left foot. Your torso turns northeast. Hold your right thigh parallel to the floor; your right foot, pointing east, tucked under it. (71a-2) Your right foot kicks eastward. Both hands move outward on a vertical plane, aligning themselves horizontally at eye level, palms outward.

72. BRUSH KNEE AND PUNCH OPPONENT'S PUBIC REGION

72a. Brush Knee

(72a) Your right foot retracts and, (72a-1) pointing southeast, steps east and carries your weight. Your left palm, turning downward, sweeps across at eye level to your right shoulder line, forearm parallel to the floor, fingers pointing southeast. Your right fist, palm upward, moves to your right side. (72a-2) Your left foot, pointing east, steps east. Your left hand sweeps down to hip level on your left shoulder line, palm facing north.

72b. Punch Opponent's Pubic Region

(72b) Shift to your left foot. Your left palm faces downward near your left thigh. Your right fist strikes eastward at groin level, your palm turning at the last moment to face north. Keep your head up.

73. GRASP BIRD'S TAIL, FOLLOW UP, PUSH UP, PULL BACK, PRESS FORWARD AND PUSH

Repeat nos. 25a to 25b, 2b-2 to 2e-1 (not shown here). However, as you push up, draw your rear foot in a half step; before you press forward, step out a half step with your lead foot. This is called the follow up.

74. SINGLE WHIP, SNAKE CREEPS DOWN

Repeat nos. 3a to 3a-6, 54b to 54b-3 (not shown here).

75. STEP UP TO FORM SEVEN STARS

(75a) Point your left foot southwest and shift to it. Your left hand extends, fingers pointing west, palm facing upward. Point your right foot northwest. Your open right hand swings down toward your right hip, palm facing downward, fingers pointing west. (75a-1) Your right foot steps direct-

63a-4

71a

72a-1

ly west, only the ball of your foot being placed down one-half step in front of your left foot. Both hands and arms extend out, your wrists crossing at eye level over your center line, palms facing downward, hands closed into fists. Your torso faces directly west. Your eyes look west also.

76. RETREAT TO RIDE THE TIGER

(76a) Your right foot, pointing northwest, steps back. Both hands open. Your torso turns slightly to the left. Your left arm is parallel to the floor, your left hand held at shoulder level on your left shoulder line. Your right hand lowers down your left shoulder line to a hip-level position beneath your left forearm. Both palms face downward. (76a-1) Your weight shifts to your right foot. Your torso turns to the right. Both hands move across to your right shoulder line. (76a-2) Coming up on its ball, your left foot pulls back to a spot one-half step in front of your right. Your left hand sweeps down your right shoulder line to hip level, then crosses at hip level, ending up one foot to the outside of your left thigh, palm facing downward, fingers pointing west. Your right hand sweeps directly north and up to throat level, palm facing north, fingers pointing west. (76a-3) Your torso turns to the left and faces directly west. For further visual clarification, see no. 86.

77. TURN AROUND AND POSITION THE LOTUS

77a. Turn Around

(77a to 77a-4) The movements here are identical to those in nos. 41a to 41a-4 except for the placement of your hands. Here, your left hand comes up to shoulder level, palm facing downward. Your right hand, palm facing downward, sweeps down directly underneath your left hand at hip level. Both hands are on your center line. Your left foot lifts up and sweeps down and behind you. Pivoting on the ball of your right foot, you are going to spin around 360 degrees. Leaving your hands and arms as they are, your left foot kicks out low and around in a clockwise circle. Your left foot, pointing southwest, ends up one-half step behind your pivoting right foot. Your torso faces west with your hands held in before you. Your weight shifts to your left foot. Your right foot, pointing west, comes up on its ball. Your eyes look west.

77b. Position the Lotus

(77b) By turning your hips to the left as far as possible, swing your right foot to the left as high and as far as you can. Turn your torso to the right as far as possible. Your eyes look at your hands. (77b-1) Your right leg and foot sweep across from left to right at chest level or higher. Your hands sweep across from right to left, striking the top of your right foot when they meet at your center line. Your eyes look at your hands.

76a

76a·1

76a·2

77a

77a·1

77a·2

77a·4

77b

77b·1

78. SHOOT TIGER WITH DRAWN BOW

78a

(78a) Your hands follow through to the left. Your right foot sweeps through to the right. (78a-1) Your right foot, pointing northwest, steps northwest. Both hands, closed into fists, sweep across at shoulder level and end before you, palms facing northwest. Your head and torso face northwest. Shift to your right foot. (78a-2) Your torso turns north. Both fists withdraw toward your chest. (78a-3) Your torso turns northwest. Your left fist, palm facing northwest, strikes directly to the southwest at armpit level. Your right fist, palm facing northwest also, rises up toward your right temple. Keep your right elbow lower than your right fist. Your eyes look southwest.

79. DEFLECT SIDEWAYS, PARRY, STEP UP AND PUNCH

78a-3

(79a) Your head turns to the right and your eyes look to the northwest. Your right arm extends to the northwest, your right fist opening, palm facing northwest, fingertips held at eye level. Your left fist opens and your left palm moves to face your right elbow. (79a-1) Your weight shifts to your left foot. Both hands pull down and swing over to your left side at hip level. Your eyes look directly west. (79a-2) Your left palm turns to face upward. Your right arm swings up parallel to the floor, forearm pointing southwest, hand closed into a fist, palm facing downward. Your right leg lifts up until its thigh is parallel to the floor and your right foot is tucked under your right thigh. Continue by repeating the movements of nos. 11a-2 to 11c-1 as shown earlier (not pictured here).

80. APPARENT COUNTER AND CLOSURE

Repeat the movements of nos. 12a to 12b as shown earlier (not pictured here).

81. CROSS HANDS

Repeat the movements of nos. 13a to 13a-4 as shown earlier (not pictured here).

82. END OF TAI CHI

82a

(82a) Your left foot comes together with your right. At the same time, both palms come in and turn downward, pivoting around your wrists until both arms form a rectangle parallel to the floor at shoulder level. Your right forearm, pointing west, is on top of your left forearm, pointing east. Breathe in. (82a-1) Your right hand falls from your left shoulder line down and across your torso to your right shoulder line and ends at hip level, palm facing the floor, fingers pointing north. Your left hand falls from your right shoulder line down and across your torso to your left shoulder line and ends at hip level, palm facing downward, fingers pointing north. Breathe out. (82a-2) Your palms turn to face your thighs. Your eyes look directly north. Relaxation should now be total.

78a·1

78a·2

79a

79a·1

79a·2

82a·1

82a·2

83

85a·1

CLARIFYING PHOTOGRAPHS

(83) Grasp Bird's Tail—Left. (84) White Stork Displays its Wings. (85a through 85b) Hit Tiger Left and Right. (86) Retreat to Ride the Tiger.

85b·2

84

85a

85a·2

85b

85b·1

85b·3

86

D. TAI CHI'S TWENTY-FOUR — THE SHORT YANG

Tai Chi's 24 is a condensed version of Tai Chi's 82 movements. Tai Chi's 82 movements are composed of 32 basic forms. Tai Chi's 24 is composed of 75 percent of the basic forms. It was designed to serve four principal functions. They are as follows:

1. It was designed for those who did not have the time to practice the long form, but still wished to gain the benefits from the practice of Tai Chi Chuan.
2. It was designed for the old and the elderly people who were learning Tai Chi Chuan for the first time and who would have found learning the long form too strenuous.
3. It was designed for all hospital patients who needed some form of psychophysical therapy.
4. It was designed for anyone with special physical disabilities who wanted to practice some form of physical therapy.

1. THE NAMES AND THE ORDER OF THE TWENTY-FOUR FORMS

The numbers of the movements from 1-174 are separated and related to the names of the forms from 1-24. This is done to help those of you who have the Chinese chart and diagram on the Short Form of Tai Chi Chuan.

	Movements
1. The Beginning of Tai Chi	1-4
2. Parting of Wild Horse's Mane Left	5-9
Parting of Wild Horse's Mane Right	10-14
Parting of Wild Horse's Mane Left	15-19
3. White Stork Displays Its Wings	20-22
4. Brush Knee and Twist Left	23-27
Brush Knee and Twist Right	28-32
Brush Knee and Twist Left	33-37
5. Play Guitar	38-40
6. Fall Back and Twist Like Monkey Right	41-44
Fall Back and Twist Like Monkey Left	45-47
Fall Back and Twist Like Monkey Right	48-50

■

chapter IV_____

IV. TRANSLATIONS FROM THE CHINESE

A. RULES OF PRACTICE
B. RULES OF THE BODY
C. TEN ESSENTIAL POINTS

A. RULES OF PRACTICE

1. Do not exert force.
2. Flow the mind; flow the chi.
3. Walk like a cat.
4. Up and down follow each other.
5. Breathe naturally.
6. Be continuous like one uniform thread hung together.
7. Any change comes from the waist and hips.
8. Chi should flow to the four limbs.
9. Determine the difference between soft and hard.
10. All movements should be circular.

B. RULES OF THE BODY

1. Raise the spirit.
2. Strength comes from the ability to be humble, sensitive and receptive.
3. Expand the chest and raise the back.
4. Concentrate the breathing on the psychic navel center.
5. Hands and shoulders should be level.
6. Pelvis, knees and hips should be loose, relaxed and level.
7. Coccyx (tail bone) should be straight.
8. Lumbar area (lower spine) should be straight.
9. Inside and outside should be equally balanced.

C. TEN ESSENTIAL POINTS

1. Strength comes from the ability to be humble, sensitive and receptive.
2. Expand the chest; raise the back.
3. Relax the waist and the hips.
4. Determine the difference between soft and hard.
5. Lower the shoulders and bend the arms.
6. Let the mind lead the muscles, not vice versa.
7. Up and down follow each other.
8. Inside and outside should be equally balanced.
9. Movement is continuous without break.
10. From motion you obtain serenity and stability.

■

chapter V_____

V. THE ART OF JOIN—STICK—PUSH HANDS

A. INTRODUCTION
B. GENERAL PRINCIPLES AND RULES
C. SECTION ONE: THE SIMPLE BASIC PRACTICE METHOD
   FORMS OF THE ART OF JOIN—STICK—PUSH HANDS
   WITH FIXED STEPS
   1. The Art of Joined Hands Applying the Techniques of
      Pushing and Neutralizing with One Hand
   2. The Art of Sticking Hands Applying the Techniques "Stick"
      and "Stick and Raise" Describing a Level Horizontal Circle
      with Two Hands
   3. The Art of Pushing Hands Applying the Techniques of Push
      and Pull with Two Hands
   4. The Art of Joined Hands Applying the Technique of the
      Single Pull with Two Hands
   5. The Art of Sticking Hands Applying the Techniques of
      Pushing and Neutralizing with Two Hands
   6. The Art of Pushing Hands Applying the Techniques of
      Pulling and Pressing Forward with Two Hands
   7. The Art of Joined Hands Applying the Techniques and
      Forms of "Fold" and "Pile" with Two Hands
   8. The Art of Pushing Hands Describing a Vertical Circle and
      Applying the Techniques and the Forms of the Monkey, the
      Stork and the Snake with One Hand
D. SECTION TWO: THE FOUR HANDS APPLICATION OF THE
   TECHNIQUES OF PUSH UP, PULL BACK, PRESS FOR-
   WARD AND PUSH OF THE ART OF JOIN—STICK—PUSH
   HANDS WITH FIXED STEPS

V. THE ART OF JOIN—STICK—PUSH HANDS

A. INTRODUCTION

1. Join—Stick—Push Hands is divided into four main sections as follows:

Section One   The simple basic practice method forms of the Art of Join—Stick—Push Hands with fixed steps

Section Two	The four hand application of the techniques of Push Up, Pull Back, Press Forward and Push of the Art of Join—Stick—Push Hands with fixed steps
Section Three	The four hand application of the techniques of Push Up, Pull Back, Press Forward and Push of the Art of Join—Stick—Push Hands with active steps
Section Four	TA LU—Long Pull Back or Great Repulse

Each succeeding section is established on the knowledge of the preceding sections. Section one, therefore, forms the foundation for section two. Sections one and two form the foundation for section three. Sections one, two and three form the foundation for section four. You must always begin at section one and work your way up to section four. You must never work backwards from section four to section one. If you ever hope to comprehend the meaning and significance of softness in its relationship to meditation or to gain proficiency in the martial art aspect of Tai Chi Chuan, you must thoroughly understand and comprehend both the theory and the application of the principles of each section before proceeding on to the next.

2. The Art of Join—Stick—Push Hands is the FOUNDATION for the understanding of SOFTNESS and its relationship to MEDITATION. It is relatively easy to become fluid and soft while doing Tai Chi's Eighty-Two. It is another matter to be fluid and soft when you are directly in contact with another person. In other words, if you can be soft and fluid in Join—Stick—Push Hands with a person, then you will know the meaning of fluidity and softness with another human being. You will experience fluidity (naturalness and spontaneity) and softness (sensitivity and tenderness) in relationship.

B. GENERAL PRINCIPLES AND RULES

1. Advance — Retreat

    (1) When an opponent advances, you must retreat.

When an opponent retreats, you must advance.

(2) On general principle, all strikes and attacks are executed with the advances; all parries and blocks are executed with the retreats.

Advance	Retreat
Forward	Backward
Towards	Away From
Focus	Relax
Hard	Soft
Male	Female
Strike	Parry

2. Pressure Relating to Touch and Sensitivity

    (1) *Four Do's*
        a. Stick
        b. Stick and Raise
        c. Join
        d. Follow-Through

    (2) *Four Don't's*
        a. Oppose
        b. Separate
        c. Divide
        d. Resist

3. Retreat and Then Turn

Do not turn first and then retreat. Retreat first and then execute the parry or block with a turn of your torso. Remember to shift before turning.

4. Center Line

This is the plane that divides you equally into left and right sides. Always strike alongside or right down your center line. Parry or block from the shoulder line across the center line to the shoulder line.

Do not block beyond the shoulder line or head line. After striking, return the hands and feet to a coiled position. After all parries, return the hands and feet to the center line.

5. Push—Pull

When an opponent pushes, you pull with the push.
When an opponent pulls, you push with the pull.

6. Grabbing and Catching a Limb (Locking, twisting, breaking)

   Execute the parry or block. As soon as you have made contact, turn your wrist, hook over, and catch the limb.
   Parry—Contact—Turn—Catch—Pull = Lock—Twist or Break.

7. Striking and Parrying

   Strikes may be either straight or round; parries must be round. In no way must a block be executed straight, otherwise it will be a hard block. Hard blocks reflect poor parrying techniques in Tai Chi Chuan.

8. Look to the Left and Look to the Right (Turn Left and Turn Right)

   When you strike out with the left or right hand, follow it with your eyes. When you pull down with the left or right hand, follow it with your eyes. In other words, you must always look in the direction toward which you are exerting your force. For instance, you would not throw someone over your shoulder and simultaneously be looking at him. You would be looking in the direction in which you are throwing him. If you observe someone following these rules when he practices Tai Chi, you will see that whenever the eyes follow the hands or feet, the head turns. Whichever way the head turns, the hips and torso will follow. The total effect is to bring into play all the muscles of the body, putting maximum power into your thrust or pull.

9. Be Always in Motion (Be Fluid)

   You must always be shifting your weight from one foot to the other. You must learn never to overextend or underextend. You learn to move from a forward stance to a back stance and vice versa. You learn never to be double-weighted. You learn to turn and twist your torso properly with each shift. You learn coordination of the whole physical self, but it is even more important to learn to maintain perfect posture and balance in motion. Never be still. Be fluid and always in motion.

C. SECTION ONE: THE SIMPLE BASIC PRACTICE METHOD FORMS OF THE ART OF JOIN—STICK—PUSH HANDS WITH FIXED STEPS

Section one is divided into eight sub-sections. As you practice them with your partner, you will notice that number two (the art of sticking hands applying the techniques "stick" and "stick and raise" describing a level horizontal circle with two hands) is an extension of number one (the art of joined hands applying the techniques of pushing and neutralizing with one hand); that number three (the art of pushing hands applying the techniques of push and pull with two hands) is an extension of number one combined with number two; that number four (the art of joined hands applying the technique of the single pull with two hands) is an extension and variation of number three; that number five is an extension of number two; that number six is an extension and variation of number three and number four; that number seven is a variation of number five; and that number eight is an extension and variation of number one. In the final analysis, each sub-section is based on number one. Number one is the key to understanding the meaning and the significance of the circle, its application and its uses in the Art of Join—Stick—Push Hands practice.

1. THE ART OF JOINED HANDS APPLYING THE TECH-NIQUES OF PUSHING AND NEUTRALIZING WITH ONE HAND

(1) Clarification

    a. Footwork: If A steps out with his right foot, B steps out with his right foot. If A steps out with his left foot, B steps out with his left foot.

    b. Shifting: When A advances and shifts forward into a forward stance, B automatically retreats and shifts back into a back stance. When A advances, B retreats. When B advances, A retreats.

    (a) Forward Shift (Advance): Use attacking techniques of push, push up and press forward.

    (b) Backward Shift (Retreat): Use defensive techniques of deflect to the left/look to the left, deflect to the right/look to the right, pull back and neutralize.

    c. Handwork

A (Advance)	B (Retreat)
(a) Push	Turn to deflect left

(b) Push	Turn to deflect right
(c) Push up	Pull back
(d) Press forward	Neutralize
A (Retreat)	B (Advance)
(e) Deflect to the left	Push
(f) Deflect to the right	Push
(g) Pull back	Push up
(h) Neutralize	Press forward

(2) Beginning Position

A, with his right elbow down and body in a back stance, places his right palm, fingers up, against B's right wrist. B takes a forward stance. B's forearm is parallel to the floor. B's right palm faces B's chest.

(3) Movement

As A pushes, B turns and deflects a quarter of a circle to the left. Now B has moved a quarter of a circle to the left and a half shift back. A continues to push. B turns and deflects a quarter of a circle to the right. As A feels the turn of B's wrist to B's right, A counters the deflection with the push up technique. A pushes up by turning his wrist until his palm faces his own chest, his forearm coming parallel to the floor. B counters the push up with the pull back technique. As B deflects up with his right wrist, B catches A's right wrist and pulls back and down with it. A counters the pull back with the press forward. B counters the press forward with the neutralize technique which is B's body retreating and giving way with both arms and legs to the force exerted by A's right forearm. Now A has completely advanced and B has shifted back as far as possible. The ending position for A and B is the reverse of their beginning position. Now B advances using A's advance techniques and A retreats using B's retreat techniques.

When you deflect to the right, turn your torso to the right and look to the right. When you deflect to the left, turn your torso to the left and look to your left.

You can see that one entire advance and retreat cycle completes one whole circle. That circle contains nine basic techniques executed in the following order: (1) push,

(2) push up, (3) press forward, (4) deflect left, (5) look to the left, (6) deflect up to the right, (7) look to the right, (8) pull back and (9) neutralize. "Deflect left" and "look to the left," "deflect up to the right" and "look to the right," and "look to the right" and "pull back" are executed simultaneously. They are inseparable.

You draw the circle first with your right hand and foot out. Then, you do it with your left hand and right foot out. Then, you do it with your left foot and left hand out. Then, you do it with your right hand and left foot out.

2. THE ART OF STICKING HANDS APPLYING THE TECHNIQUES "STICK" AND "STICK AND RAISE" DESCRIBING A LEVEL HORIZONTAL CIRCLE WITH TWO HANDS

The seven sub-sections which begin here and run through number eight (the art of pushing hands describing a vertical circle and applying the techniques and the forms of the monkey, the stork and the snake with one hand) are merely extensions, variations or combinations of the techniques used in number one. If you have any difficulty with these later sub-sections, return to number one. Number one holds all the secrets, and all the techniques of Join—Stick—Push Hands lie in its circle.

Number two is an extension of number one.

(1) Clarification

  a. Footwork: A steps out with his right foot. B steps out with his right foot.

  b. Shifting: When A advances, B retreats. When B advances, A retreats.

  c. Handwork

A (Advance)	B (Retreat)
(a) Push up	Neutralize
A (Retreat)	B (Advance)
(b) Neutralize	Push

(2) Beginning Position

  Begin as in number one except that B has both hands on A's forearm. B's left palm, fingers pointing up, is against A's right elbow. B's right palm, fingers pointing up, is against A's right wrist. A's forearm is parallel to the floor, right palm facing his own chest. A's left hand, palm up, is touching B's right elbow. A is in a right forward stance. B is in a left back stance.

(3) Movement

A pushes up and extends his right forearm. B stays in touch but gives way. B pushes back and A gives way to B. As they are shifting back and forth, A draws a circle as he pushes up. After a while, A and B change hand positions. B takes the push up arm position and A takes the push hand position. After a while, they change their feet around and push up with the left arm.

Pushing up with the arm may be practiced in four ways: with the right arm and right foot leading; or with the right arm and left foot leading; or with the left arm and left foot leading; or with the left arm and right foot leading.

3. THE ART OF PUSHING HANDS APPLYING THE TECHNIQUES OF PUSH AND PULL WITH TWO HANDS

Number three is a combination of numbers one and two.

(1) Clarification
   a. Footwork: A steps out with his right foot. B steps out with his right foot.

   b. Shifting: When A advances, B retreats. When B advances, A retreats.

   c. Handwork

A (Advance)	B (Retreat)
(a) Push	Neutralize
(b) Push	Deflect up to the right
(c) Push up	Pull back
(d) Press forward	Neutralize

(2) Beginning Position

B's right forearm is parallel to the floor. B's right palm faces B's chest. B's left hand is placed on his right bicep. B's left elbow is held pointing downward. A's right palm, fingers pointing up, is placed against B's right wrist. A's left palm, fingers pointing up, is placed against B's right elbow. This position is the same as that of number two except that B's left hand is on his right bicep. B is in a right forward stance. A is in a left back stance.

(3) Movement

As A pushes against B's forearm, B retreats directly. A continues the push. B counters by deflecting up to the right. B must execute this technique before he has retreated more than half way. A counters the deflection to the right by executing the push up technique. B counters the push up with the pull back technique. A counters the pull back with the press forward technique. B counters the press forward with the neutralize technique. Now, the positions have been reversed. B is in A's beginning position and A is in B's beginning position. Now B advances and A retreats.

Remember the main dictum—retreat, then turn. There is a tendency for students to deflect to the left first, as in number one, but there is no deflection to the left. Second, be sure to retreat and give way first before you deflect to the right. There is also a tendency for most students to turn right away without retreating directly and giving way to pressure, first.

You can practice number three as you did number one: with your right foot out and your right arm in the push up position; or with your right foot out and your left arm in the push up position; or with your left foot out and your left arm in the push up position; or with your left foot out and your right arm in the push up position.

You have just learned to do number three pushing with both hands against the wrist and elbow. Now, do it in the four different positions but push differently. You do not pull back the opponent's arm so that his elbow is in line with one of your shoulder lines and his wrist is in line with your other shoulder line. Instead, you pull back until his wrist is beyond your shoulder line and his elbow is in line with your center line. Now, push against the elbow with one hand and touch only his wrist with your other hand. All of the pressure is applied to your opponent's elbow.

Practice number three both ways. First, apply pressure evenly to both the wrist and the elbow. Then, apply it only to the elbow.

4. THE ART OF JOINED HANDS APPLYING THE TECH-
   NIQUE OF THE SINGLE PULL WITH TWO HANDS

Number four is an extension and variation of number three.

(1) Clarification

    a. Footwork: A steps out with his right foot. B steps out with his right foot.

    b. Shifting: When A advances, B retreats. When B advances, A retreats.

    c. Handwork

A (Retreat)	B (Advance)
(a) Pull	Push up
(b) Neutralize	Press forward

A (Advance)	B (Retreat)
(c) Push up	Pull
(d) Press forward	Neutralize

(2) Beginning Position

A takes a right forward stance. B takes a left back stance. A's right arm is in the press forward position and B is in a push position. The beginning position here is identical to the ending movements in number three.

(3) Movement

A turns his right wrist, catches hold of B's right wrist and pulls. B counters the pull technique with a push up technique. A continues to pull. B counters with the press forward technique. A counters by giving way (neutralizing), by bending both elbows and giving way with both arms. Now, B does what A has done. A does what B has just done.

The main thing to remember is that, unlike numbers one, two and three, the person in the forward stance here initiates the movement. Also, the press forward is a very short and fine movement to be used only when your push up arm is as close to your opponent's body as it can be without your losing your balance. Also, the neutralize counter-technique is a very short and fine movement.

The only difference between the push up and the press

forward is direction. The press forward technique is merely the push up arm turned into the opponent's center after he has pulled back and deflected your push up arm to the side.

5. THE ART OF STICKING HANDS APPLYING THE TECHNIQUES OF PUSHING AND NEUTRALIZING WITH TWO HANDS

Number five is merely an extension and variation of number two combined with number three.

(1) Clarification

    a. Footwork: A steps forward with his right foot. B steps forward with his right foot.

    b. Shifting: When A advances, B retreats. When B advances, A retreats.

    c. Handwork

A (Advance)	B (Retreat)
(a) Push	Deflect to the left
A (Retreat)	B (Advance)
(b) Deflect to the left	Push

(2) Beginning Position

A is in a left back stance. B is in a right forward stance. A's arms are in a push position. B's arms are in a push up position. Their arms are in the same position as in number two.

(3) Movement

As A advances and pushes, B retreats directly until he is one-half shift back. Then, B deflects A's hands to the left. At this point, B is in a left back stance and A is in a right forward stance. A must keep his hands in touch with B's right wrist and elbow. B must keep his weight on his left foot. Now B, drawing a vertical circle with his hands, flips A's right arm over into a push up position by turning with his hips and waist to the right. B ends up in a push position with his hands on A's right wrist and right elbow. Now you have completed a half circle. Now B advances and pushes. A retreats and deflects first to his left, then flips B's right arm over to the right.

The two main things to remember are first to retreat directly before deflecting to the left. Do not turn first and then shift. Give way to pressure directly first. Then deflect the pressure to the side by turning to the left. Also, remember as you flip your opponent's arm to the right, your weight must be on your back foot. You turn to the right by concentrating on the turn of your hips and waist. Throughout the movement, A and B always have both hands on each other's wrist and elbow.

There are two positions in which to practice: with your right arm in the push up position and your right foot out; and with your left arm in the push up position and your left foot out (as in number two).

6. THE ART OF PUSHING HANDS APPLYING THE TECHNIQUES OF PULLING AND PRESSING FORWARD WITH TWO HANDS

Number six is an extension and variation and combination of numbers three and four.

(1) Clarification

    a. Footwork: A steps forward with his right foot. B steps forward with his right foot.

    b. Shifting: When A advances, B retreats. When B advances, A retreats.

    c. Handwork

A (Advance)	B (Retreat)
(a) Press forward	Deflect to the side
(b) Push up	Pull back
(c) Press forward	Neutralize

A (Retreat)	B (Advance)
(d) Deflect to the side	Press forward
(e) Pull back	Push up
(f) Neutralize	Press forward

(2) Beginning Position

A is in a left back stance. B is in a right forward stance.

A's hands are in a push position. B's left arm is in a push up position.

(3) Movement

The press forward arm tactic is the same form shown in Tai Chi's 82, the solo exercise. A places his right wrist over B's left elbow with A's right arm parallel to the floor. A places his left palm, fingers pointing straight up, on his right wrist, advances and presses forward against B's left elbow, aiming his attack down B's center line. As A advances, B retreats directly, but only with a slight shift back. B drops his left elbow straight down, turns his left palm to face him, left fingers pointing straight up and out, and deflects A's right arm to his (B's) left side. A counters the deflection of his right arm by firing his left arm, in a push up position, at B. B turns his left palm outward and catches A's push up arm at the elbow and wrist with his (B's) left palm against A's left wrist and his right palm against A's left elbow. B pulls on A's left arm and A counters by pushing up and in towards B's center, which is called the press forward technique, as in number four. Now A and B have completed a half circle. A is now in B's beginning position and B is in A's beginning position.

In number six, there are only two positions for practice: with the right foot leading and the left arm in a push up position, and with the left foot leading and the right arm in a push up position.

7. THE ART OF JOINED HANDS APPLYING THE TECHNIQUES AND FORMS OF "FOLD" AND "PILE" WITH TWO HANDS

Number seven is just a variation of number five. However, instead of pushing with your palms, you flip your palms over the opponent's wrist and elbow. With both palms facing the ceiling, you push against the opponent's arm with your wrists. You are attacking with your fingertips and defending with fishtail blocks. This is the only, but significant, difference between numbers five and seven.

8. THE ART OF PUSHING HANDS DESCRIBING A VERTICAL CIRCLE AND APPLYING THE TECHNIQUES AND

THE FORMS OF THE MONKEY, THE STORK AND THE SNAKE WITH ONE HAND

Number eight is an extension and variation of number one.

(1) Clarification

    a. Footwork: A steps out with his right foot. B steps out with his right foot.

    b. Shifting: When A advances, B retreats. When B advances, A retreats.

    c. Handwork

A (Advance)	B (Retreat)
(a) Monkey's palm strikes out	White stork parries
A (Retreat)	B (Advance)
(b) Monkey parries	Snake strikes

(2) Beginning Position

A takes a left back stance. A has the back of his right wrist on top of B's right wrist. A's right hand is opened, palm facing up, fingers pointing forward. A's right hand is against his right side from waist to hip level. A's left hand and arm are hanging down his left side. B takes a forward stance. B's right hand and arm are in a push up position. B's arm is between A's hip and waist level. B's left arm is hanging down his left side.

(3) Movement

As A advances, A's right hand turns 180 degrees and A's palm strikes out at B's face. As A advances, B retreats and deflects A's right palm strike over to the side of B's right temple. B's right palm turns 180 degrees. B's right palm, initially facing him, now faces away from his right temple. B's blocking movement is the same as the parrying motion in the White Stork Spreads Its Wings movement in Tai Chi's 82.

A is now in a right forward stance and B is in a left back stance. With his right hand, B pulls A's arm down to B's right side between hip and waist level. B's right palm faces the floor. A's right hand and arm are now in a push up position. A's right palm has turned to face him. As B advances, B turns his right hand one quarter of a circle, and strikes out at A's solar plexus with a spear hand. A retreats and parries by pulling back and against B's wrist and forearm with his right wrist and forearm and by turning his right palm one quarter of a circle until his palm (A's) faces up on his right side between waist and hip level.

Each side has advanced and retreated once, completing a circle. Both sides have drawn a complete vertical circle. A and B can change hand positions so that B can practice A's hand techniques and A can practice B's hand techniques. A and B can practice each of these striking and blocking techniques four ways: (1) with the right foot and right hand out, (2) with the right foot and left hand out, (3) with the left foot and right hand out, and (4) with the left foot and left hand out.

D. SECTION TWO: THE FOUR HANDS APPLICATION OF THE TECHNIQUES OF PUSH UP, PULL BACK, PRESS FORWARD AND PUSH OF THE ART OF JOIN—STICK—PUSH HANDS WITH FIXED STEPS

1. THE ART OF JOINED HANDS WITH CORRESPONDING STEPS

(1) Clarification

    a.   Footwork: If A steps out with his right foot, B steps out with his right foot. If A steps out with his left foot, B steps out with his left foot.

    b.   Handwork: You may describe a circle to the right or left, that is, clockwise or counterclockwise—depending on whether you step out with your left or right foot. When you advance, you apply the techniques push, push up and press forward. When you retreat, you apply the techniques deflect up, pull back and neutralize.

2. THE ART OF STICKING HANDS WITH OPPOSITE STEPS

(1) Clarification

a. Footwork: If A steps out with his left foot, B steps out with his right foot. If A steps out with his right foot, B steps out with his left foot. The right foot is always placed on the outside of the left foot. The left foot is always placed on the inside of the right foot.

b. Handwork: If you step out with the left foot, you describe the circle to the left. The left foot always indicates that you are to describe the circle counterclockwise. If you step out with the right foot, you describe the circle to the right. The right foot indicates that you must describe the circle clockwise. Remember—
   (a) RIGHT FOOT: CIRCLE TO THE RIGHT (CLOCKWISE)
   (b) LEFT FOOT: CIRCLE TO THE LEFT (COUNTERCLOCKWISE)

E. SECTION THREE: THE FOUR HANDS APPLICATION OF THE TECHNIQUES OF PUSH UP, PULL BACK, PRESS FORWARD AND PUSH OF THE ART OF JOIN—STICK—PUSH HANDS WITH ACTIVE STEPS

1. THE ART OF PUSHING HANDS WITH CORRESPONDING STEPS (3/3 Count)

   (1) Footwork

      a. Starting Position: If A steps forward with his right foot, B steps forward with his right foot. Both A and B face each other in a right forward stance.

      b. Movement: A shifts his weight to his rear foot and raises his right foot. B lifts his rear foot. A steps down with his right foot and shifts his weight to his right foot. His count is now one. B steps down with his rear foot. His count is now one. A steps forward with his left foot. His count is now two. B steps back with his right foot. His count is now two. A steps forward with his right foot. His count is now three. B steps back with his left foot. His count is now three.

      c. End Position: At the end of count three, both A and B face each other in a right forward stance. Now B starts forward and A retreats. A and B each take turns advancing three counts forward and three counts backward. When B advances and retreats once, A and B will have completed one round, one circle, one Yin and one Yang. Unity now gives Harmony.

All the foot movements are coordinated. Both A and B raise their feet together and place them down at the same time. But, the foot raised and the foot placed down are always opposite. That is, if A lifts his right foot, B lifts his left foot; if A drops his right foot, B drops his left foot. When you step down with the forward foot, be sure it is placed next to your opponent's foot. The forward feet of both A and B should always be placed next to each other. They should never be placed behind each other.

The above paragraph describes footwork—right style. You should also practice left style; that is, begin with the left foot forward instead of the right foot forward. If you hope to develop proficiency and overall balance in the mastery of the footwork, do both sides.

As you advance and retreat to the count of three, you must turn. At first, you will move straight backward and forward. As you progress, you will learn to turn in one direction, then the other. As you advance and retreat and turn at the same time, first clockwise, then counterclockwise, you will realize that you are moving in a circle. In the beginning, you will walk, then run in large circles. But, in the more advanced stages of training, you should be able to walk, then run, in a very tight circle. You will forever be describing the Tai Chi Circle.

While advancing and retreating, A and B are each trying to maintain control of the center of the circle. As A advances, B is driven out of the center onto the circumference. But, as B advances, A is driven out of the center onto the circumference. The Advance (Yang) and the Retreat (Yin) of both persons describe spiral radii running in both directions—clockwise and counterclockwise. The pattern will be that of a Circle (A Round Flower) with symmetrical petals radiating from the center.

(2) Handwork—Counterclockwise: A takes the "Two-Hand Push" position. A's right hand is placed on B's right wrist. A's left hand is placed on B's right elbow. On the first

count, A applies the push technique. B begins the exchange of arms by removing A's left hand, which is touching his (B's) elbow, with B's left hand. On the second count, A continues to apply the push technique. B applies the deflect up technique with his left hand against A's left wrist. On the third count, A applies the push up and press forward technique. B then applies the pull back and neutralize technique.

2. THE ART OF STICKING HANDS WITH OPPOSITE STEPS (3/2 Count)

(1) Footwork—First Movement

a. Starting Position: A steps forward with his right foot into the right forward stance. B steps forward with his left foot into the left forward stance. A's right foot should be outside B's left foot. B's left foot should be inside A's right foot.

b. First Movement (A advances and B retreats): A shifts his weight onto his left foot and raises his right foot. As A raises his right foot, B rises on the ball of his right foot. As A steps down with his right foot inside B's left foot, his count becomes one. As A steps down, B shifts his weight onto his right foot so that he is in a back stance. A steps forward with his left foot. His count is now two. B steps back with his left foot. His count is now one. A steps forward with his right foot. His count is now three. B steps back with his right foot. His count is now two.

c. End Position: A ends in a right forward stance. B ends in a left back stance.

(2) Footwork—Second Movement

a. Starting Position: The end position of the first movement is the starting position of the second. B is in a left back stance and A's right foot is on the inside of B's left foot. B's left foot is on the outside of A's right foot.

b. Second Movement (B advances and A retreats): B steps forward with his left foot inside A's right foot. His count is now one. A shifts his weight to his left foot. B steps forward with his right foot. His count is now two. A steps back with his right foot. His count is now one. B steps forward with his left foot inside A's right foot. His count is now three. A steps back with his left foot. His count is now two.

 c. End Position: B ends in a left forward stance. A ends in a right back stance.

Both A and B end in approximately the stance assumed for the starting position of the first movement. They have now completed an entire movement. By advancing and retreating once, they have completed the circle and made one whole. Yin and Yang are now complementary and harmonized.

(3) Handwork: A applies the push technique with the count of one. B exchanges arms while shifting from his forward foot to his rear foot. A applies the push technique on count two. B applies the deflect up technique on count one. A applies the push up and press forward technique on the count of three. B applies the pull back and neutralize technique with the count of two.

(4) Opposite Steps: The Reality of the Moving Pattern

The overall foot pattern is a circle going in only one direction—counterclockwise. In actual fact, the person with his left foot out moves counterclockwise while his hands move clockwise; the person with his right foot out moves clockwise while his hands move counterclockwise.

3. A COMPARISON OF CORRESPONDING STEPS TO OPPO-SITE STEPS

(1) Similarities

 Advance — Apply Techniques "Push Up, Push and Press Forward."
 Retreat — Apply Techniques "Deflect Up, Pull Back and Neutralize."
 Advance — Three—Three Count
 Advance and Retreat — Two—Two and One-Half Steps

(2) Differences

 In corresponding steps the person who retreats must lift

his rear foot off the ground before beginning his retreat.

In opposite steps the person who retreats must never lift his rear foot off the ground. He merely shifts his weight on the forward foot and comes up on the ball of his rear foot, and then quickly shifts his weight onto the rear foot.

In corresponding steps, whether starting with the left or right foot, the opponents may circle counterclockwise or clockwise with their hands with the left or right foot out.

In opposite steps the opponents may circle counterclockwise with their hands if they have the right foot out. They may circle clockwise with their hands only if they have their left foot out.

Corresponding Steps — Retreat — Three—Three Count.
Opposite Steps — Retreat — Three—Two Count.

F. SECTION FOUR:
TA LU —
LONG PULL BACK IN A FIXED PATTERN
OR GREAT REPULSE IN A RANDOM PATTERN

1. INTRODUCTION

The Ta Lu is the fourth and final section on the Art of Pushing Hands. The Ta Lu combines in one pattern all the hand and foot techniques learned in the previous three sections of the Art of Join—Stick—Push Hands. Therefore, the practice of the Ta Lu should never be neglected and should be done earnestly. If you find difficulty in doing the Ta Lu, it means that you have not really properly learned something that you should have learned in the previous three sections. The Ta Lu therefore is the corrective exercise section in the Art of Join—Stick—Push Hands. The Ta Lu checks to see that you really understand and are able to apply the theory, principles and techniques that you have learned not only from the previous three sections but also from the formal exercise, Tai Chi's 82.

Another reason for the development and practice of the Ta Lu is to use it as a connecting link into the applications, Tai Chi's 88. The Ta Lu is also used to introduce the student to several new techniques. One new footwork technique, three new hand-striking techniques, two forearm techniques, one elbow technique and one shoulder technique are added to the techniques already learned.

The new hand-striking techniques are:

(1) Palm Thrust (variation of Section One, Subsection Number Eight Form of Simple Basic Practice Methods)
(2) Forearm Smash (two variations—Smash to the Elbow; Smash to the Head or Neck)
(3) Wrist-Pull (variation of Pull Back technique)
(4) Arm-Chop (variation and extension of Pull Back technique)
(5) Elbowing
(6) Shouldering

The new hand-striking techniques are really extensions and variations of the techniques used in Section One, Simple Basic Practice Method Forms, and are always used in conjunction with the new footwork technique, which is really a variation of the forward advance of the active steps, the walking or running steps of three—three, three—two. These new techniques introduce the student to the applications, Tai Chi's 88, since these new techniques are used in the applications.

2. CIRCLE AND FOUR SIDES

The four sides are the techniques Push Up, Pull Back, Press Forward and Push. The circle refers to the movements. The four sides or techniques are rolled into a circle and the walking and running of Tai Chi is practiced in a circular pattern.

3. SQUARE AND FOUR CORNERS

(1) Ta Lu Fixed Pattern

The footwork forms four corners. When connected together the four corners form the shape of a square. The four corners also refer to the four techniques Wrist-pull, Arm-chop, Elbow, Shoulder.

(2) The movements are more angular in that they are complete movements. The technique is actually carried through and finished. The forms are not rolled into a circle and made indistinguishable but are drawn into END forms and become quite recognizable.

The Circle is for Intensity. The basic four techniques, Push Up, Pull Back, Press Forward and Push, are rolled into a circle and made indistinguishable. Any straight line force trying to enter a moving circle, such as a strong revolving wheel, is easily expelled and deflected or else sucked into the circle, as a whirlpool sucks in debris. The sucked-in force can then be flung out and turned back onto its source like a rock being fired out of a twirling sling shot. Thus the circle is for intensity, the intensity of gathering the force of the opponent, adding your force to it and sending it back onto the opponent.

The Square is for Development. The basic four techniques (the four corners), Wrist-pull, Arm-chop, Elbowing and Shouldering, cannot be applied in the Ta Lu unless you fully understand how the four techniques (four sides) of Push Up, Pull Back, Press Forward and Push are arranged and applied in the circle. If you know and understand this, then you will be able to draw the end forms from the circle. In other words, you will know how to draw your opponent's force into the circle, take that force, split it, divide it or draw it out again and turn it back against your opponent. Drawing it out of the circle is to make it angular and square. The footwork describes a square pattern. Inside that square pattern you are applying the power of the circle with your hands and body. Thus, the saying: The Circle Is For Intensity and the Square Is For Development.

4. THE TEST OF SOFTNESS

The Ta Lu movements are completed forms, executed forms, end forms, finished forms. You can see the four techniques, Push Up, Pull Back, Press Forward and Push, clearly applied, and completed including the six new techniques of Palm Thrust, Forearm Smash, Wrist-pull, Elbowing, Shouldering and Arm-twisting.

It is easy enough to be soft and describe a circle walking and running in the four hand practice, but the real test of this softness is to be able to remain soft and relax when the circle is partially broken or completely broken and drawn into a final form, that is, when the circle changes to a square. In the square, the hidden forms are drawn out of the circle and shown clearly as end forms. The circular techniques are executed to their completion; the end forms are clearly distinguishable. In other words, the real test of softness is your ability to complete each movement, draw it from the circle and take from it a technique, and to complete that technique as you do in the Simple Basic Practice Method Forms of Section One in the Art of Join—Stick—Push Hands.

You must remember that the pattern of footwork in the Ta Lu essentially describes a square and that all the shouldering techniques and elbowing techniques and palm strikes are to the corners. Therefore the Ta Lu is also referred to as the SQUARE AND THE FOUR CORNERS. Inside the pattern is the pattern of the Circle. Inside the Circle is embodied all the fine hand techniques. Therefore we again end by saying: The Circle Is For Intensity and The Square Is For Development.

TA LU: LONG PULL BACK, GREAT REPULSE

(THE SQUARE AND THE FOUR CORNERS)

The Natural Necessary Evolution Of The Sections Of The Art Of Join—Stick—Push Hands

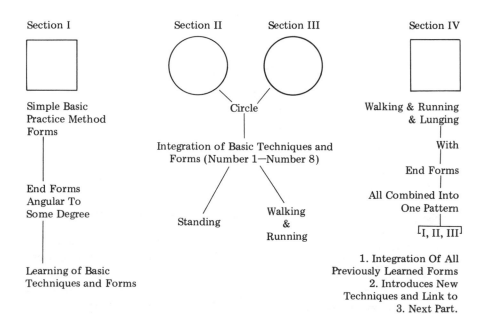

Section I

Simple Basic
Practice Method
Forms

End Forms
Angular To
Some Degree

Learning of Basic
Techniques and Forms

Section II   Section III

Circle

Integration of Basic Techniques and
Forms (Number 1—Number 8)

Standing   Walking
&
Running

Section IV

Walking & Running
& Lunging

With

End Forms

All Combined Into
One Pattern

I, II, III

1. Integration Of All
Previously Learned Forms
2. Introduces New
Techniques and Link to
3. Next Part.

G. THE FOUR DO'S

1. THE FOUR DO'S (and Their Poetic Definitions)
    (1) DO STICK (Fall In Love and Embrace)
    (2) DO STICK AND RAISE (Raise High and Lift Up)
    (3) DO JOIN (Sacrifice Yourself Without Reservations)
    (4) DO FOLLOW-THROUGH (When He Runs, Respond)

2. LITERAL EXPLANATIONS AND PURPOSES
    (1) STICK (JIM)

    In any struggle you must always be sure that both hands, or at least one hand, remain in contact with your opponent. In other words, Stick to Him, Hold on to Him, Cling to Him and Never Let Go of Him.

    You "Stick" to develop sensitivity of feeling. If your skin is alive and sensitive to touch, to any pressure exerted against or withdrawn from it, it will teach you to recognize in battle: (a) the direction of the opponent's force, (b) the part of the opponent's anatomy which he will use to strike you; that is, whether it will be with a left or right punch or a left or right foot kick.

    Sensitivity of touch will enable you to counter any attack and permit you to strike a counterblow against your opponent's weak side.

    (2) STICK AND RAISE (NIM)

    You use the technique "Stick" so that you may direct the opponent's force to "Raise" his center of gravity.

    If you can "Raise" the opponent's center of gravity, you can dislocate it and easily force him to lose his balance.

    (3) JOIN (LIN)

    In any struggle you must follow your opponent. If he advances, you retreat. If he retreats, you advance.

    You must learn to FLOW with your opponent's movements. If you learn to do this precisely, it means that you have reached a state of perfect union. In union there is no attack, no defense, no struggle, no conflict. Only in division can there be conflict. If you JOIN with his movements he cannot hurt you because you and he will be in perfect harmony.

(4) FOLLOW-THROUGH (CHU)

In "Sticking," "Sticking and Raising," and "Joining" with your opponent, you wear him down and expose many of his weaknesses. You must then exploit them with the appropriate follow-through techniques.

You adhere to this principle so that you will be able to attack and destroy your opponent with the specific attacking techniques most appropriate for the occasion and the circumstances.

3. A COMMENTARY

You Should Be Able To Fathom and Comprehend Man's Sensibilities and Movements.

Unless You Do, You Will Not Be Able To: Stick and Raise, Join, Stick and Follow-Through.

The Types of Exercises Developed To Teach These Techniques Of Stick, Stick and Raise, Join and Follow-Through Are Very Fine, Detailed and Intricate.

H. THE FOUR DON'T'S

1. THE FOUR DON'T'S (and Their Poetic Definitions)

(1) DON'T TOP (OPPOSE) (Come Out Of The Head)
(2) DON'T FLATTEN (SEPARATE) (Not Quite Reaching)
(3) DON'T DISPOSE (DIVIDE) (Leave Wide Open)
(4) DON'T RESIST (RESIST) (Too Much)

2. LITERAL EXPLANATIONS OF THE FOUR WEAKNESSES

(1) TOP (Oppose) (DING)

To defend oneself with a greater force than the strike of an opponent. If an opponent applies one hundred pounds of force against you, counter with one hundred pounds against him.

(2) FLATTENED (Separate) (BIN)

Not quite touching. If you do not keep in touch with your opponent, you will lose the power and sensitivity to apply the techniques Stick, Stick and Raise, Join and Follow-Through.

(3) THROW AWAY (Divide) (DISPOSE) (DEW)

To pull away completely. If you come in contact with your opponent, you disengage completely from him and run away. By doing so, you will lose your sensitivity of touch and you will not be able to apply the techniques Stick, Stick and Raise, Join and Follow-Through.

(4) RESIST (KONG)

To defend with a force almost as great as the strike from an opponent. If an opponent strikes out with a force of one hundred pounds, you counter it with a force almost as great, such as ninety-five pounds.

3. COMMENTARY:

(1) TOP   (2) FLATTEN   (3) DISPOSE   (4) RESIST
(Oppose)   (Separate)   (Divide)   (Resist)

You should know these four words because they are a sickness.

If you understand this, you will be able to Stick and Raise, Stick, Join and Follow-Through.

Otherwise, you will not understand the sensitivity of this exercise.

When you first begin, you aren't aware of the things you do wrong.

You must learn to remove these faults.

The difficult thing to do is to Stick, Stick and Raise, Join and Follow-Through.

Avoid the four weaknesses. This is the most difficult thing to accomplish.

I. SONG OF EIGHT WORDS

Push Up, Pull Back, Press Forward and Push are the rarest
    secrets in the world.
Of ten masters, even ten do not know these secrets.
If you can be light and lively and also firm and hard,
Without any doubt you will be able to — Stick, Stick and Raise,
    Join and Follow-Through.
Even more spectacularly: you will be able to Wrist-Pull,
    Arm-Chop, Elbow and Shoulder.

When you use these techniques, it will come naturally.
If you can really in theory and practice Stick,
　　　Stick and Raise, Join and Follow-Through, then
　　　you will be able to accomplish the circle without
　　　breaking it.

J. HAND FIGHTING SONG

Push Up, Pull Back, Press Forward and Push should always
　　　be taken seriously and practiced and done in earnest.
If you can advance spontaneously when your opponent retreats,
　　　and retreat spontaneously when your opponent advances,
　　　then men will have great difficulty attacking you.
Let them attack you with tremendous force.
You will be able, with only four ounces, to move
　　　one thousand pounds.
Draw them forward. Drop them into the vacuum. Enclose them.
　　　You will be able to do this easily if you apply the tech-
　　　niques Stick, Stick and Raise, Join and Follow-Through
　　　and avoid trying to apply the methods Oppose, Separate,
　　　Divide and Resist.

K. JOINED HANDS AND HUMAN RELATIONSHIP

The Joined Hands Exercise mirrors the approach of one human being to another. When one first learns the Art of Joined Hands, one will hear repeatedly from the instructors the two main principles, stick and do not resist. If one is able to do this, one will experience softness. That experience will clarify its meaning.

In the Art of Joined Hands, if one of the students experiences softness, then the other does so automatically and simultaneously. For some unexplainable reason, the experiencing must come to both or it will not come at all. For that matter, the experiencing of softness in any two-man practice in Tai Chi Chuan, not just in the Art of Joined Hands, must come simultaneously. At first this paradox confuses the student, but later he will see and understand it clearly.

Once the student has experienced softness, he will try to regain that experience of softness again. For some reason he will find that he cannot do it. No matter how hard he tries that experience eludes him. Instead of becoming softer through practice, he finds that he is actually becoming harder. He is losing his touch.

In the midst of his frustrations, he goes to the master and presents him with his problem. The master repeats to him the two main principles: stick and do not resist. The student returns once more and attacks his practice with new vigor and still he fails to surmount the problem. Once more he returns to his master. This time the master asks him to open his eyes and describe to him all that he can recall about his approach to the experience of softness and his state before and after experiencing it.

How the experiencing of softness came about is the important thing, not to know but to understand. At first, the students gave their complete attention to sticking and not resisting. They were giving their complete attention to themselves and each other's movement. They were not concerned about experiencing softness. Secondly, it did not come to them suddenly like an explosion, but quietly, fluidly, and most of all, subtly. Third, it came without their invitation, without any desire or any motive. Fourth, it came without any Self, I or Me being aware of it coming. Fifth, when one is in that state, the other is also and when one is out of that state, the other is also. The experiencing of softness and its end happens simultaneously with the two participating students.

The doing is all important because the doing brings about the end. If the end is all important, any means are used. These means are always destructive because the approach is biased and prejudiced. To Stick is to give one's complete attention and energy to another; not to Resist is to be open-minded and sensitive.

When one is experienced in the Art of Joined Hands, one can create different levels of flows deliberately. These flows bring about different experiences and also create different levels of softness. Although effort and control can create softness, the experience of true softness transcends all effort and control; then the axiom Stick and Do Not Resist becomes meaningful.

To flow with movement is to stick to it with no resistance. To resist it is to try to grasp and to gain it as a result. To resist it is to recreate in a crucible all the problems of life. The experiencing of softness is the experiencing of the timeless movement underlying every living thing within the totality of life. Softness is Communion.

■

chapter VI

VI. THE APPLICATIONS: TAI CHI'S EIGHTY-EIGHT

A. INTRODUCTION
B. GENERAL PRINCIPLES AND RULES
C. THE NAMES AND THE ORDER OF THE EIGHTY-EIGHT
   FORMS

VI. THE APPLICATIONS: TAI CHI'S EIGHTY-EIGHT

A. INTRODUCTION

The APPLICATIONS are a natural outgrowth of the integration of the solo exercise and the Art of Join—Stick—Push Hands. They contain 88 movements. These movements consist of a series of intertwining, interconnecting patterns of attack and defense. In no way does the practice of these movements deviate from Tai Chi Chuan's general principles and rules. The set pattern is designed to reinforce these general principles and rules of Softness and to add to it other new principles and techniques.

If one has mastered the Art of Join—Stick—Push Hands, one should be able to defend oneself with soft techniques. If one has not mastered this section, then the learning of the applications can still allow one to defend oneself not through soft techniques but through the techniques of Tai Chi's 88 Hard.

B. GENERAL PRINCIPLES AND RULES

1. Adhere to the general principles and rules of Tai Chi Chuan:
   (1) Psycho-Physical Relationship = The 11 Key Points
   (2) The Physical Principles of Balance and Body Mechanics

2. Adhere to the general principles and rules of the Art of Join—Stick—Push Hands.

3. Do not neglect wrist holds, breaking, gripping and exchanging.

4. Maintain proper distance.

   You should be in actual physical touch at all times with your opponent. There are approximately three movements where you are not quite in actual physical touch, but the separation of actual physical contact is only momentary. At no time must the person parrying ever be beyond actual striking distance of his opponent, otherwise his distance is incorrect.

5. Positioning

   (1) When the opponent advances, you retreat.
   When the opponent retreats, you advance.

   For every attack there is first a block with the retreat (i.e., a backward shift of one's weight onto the rear foot). Then counterattack with a shift forward: punching, kicking etcetera. Attack while advancing; defend while retreating.

(2) Minimum expenditure of energy for maximum results

Each time you reposition yourself to dodge an attack, move aside just enough to sidestep the blow. Do not overblock or dodge excessively. It is a waste of energy.

6. Area of Movement

Area of movement of the applications is restricted to a 90-degree arc for both sides or a quarter of a circle.

Yin—Female	Yang—Male
One-half Circle	One-half Circle
Defender	Attacker
Follower	Initiator

Each opponent must remain inside his half of the circle.

Each opponent must move only within one-half of his half of the circle.

7. Offensive Technique

All strikes, elbows, punches, kicks should be completely executed. There should be no half punch, half kick etcetera.

8. Defensive Technique

Execute all blocks and parries completely. No half blocks or parries permitted.

9. Focussing

Muscle contraction gives strength, power and force. To develop maximum strength in a strike you must make maximum use of your momentum gathered through the shifting of weight, the rotation of your hips and the thrust of your arms or your legs toward your opponent. By coordinating these separate movements you can bring into play all the energy and power released from these muscles and gather it all together and concentrate it into one point. This one point concentration is called FOCUSSING.

(1) Aiming Your Focus

When you strike for your target always aim beyond

and behind the target. If you only aim at the surface of the target, then the force you exert will travel and disperse only over the surface of the target. Then the force won't penetrate. If you aim beyond and behind the target, then the force of the incoming blow will be guided to penetrate through the target area.

(2) Point of Impact

Be relaxed before delivering a strike. Remember that unless there is complete and total relaxation instantly after impact, there will not be a bullwhip-like snap. There will be no proper focus. Then there will be no maximum concentration of power simultaneously on one point, the point of impact.

10. Striking and Force

Whenever you are attacking, strike as quickly as you can and then quickly withdraw the strike. The withdrawal should be as fast as, if not faster than, the strike itself. If you hit the target and permit your strike to linger, then the power of your strike will have time to spread over a large area. The shorter the time it takes to withdraw after the strike has been made, the greater the penetrating power of the strike. If executed properly, the quick, hard strike will penetrate like a needle but the slow strike is like hitting with a blunt instrument instead of a sharp one. One crushes over a large area but does not penetrate far. The other covers a small area but penetrates deeply.

The blow, punch or kick should be like the snap of a bullwhip. As the bullwhip is flipped out, the whip uncoils and flows fluidly outward until it becomes fully extended. The punch or kick should be the same. It should flow fluidly, but speedily, outward. At the height of its extension the whip snaps, crackles and pops, becoming at that point as taut and hard as a steel pole. Your whole being from head to toe should be as taut and hard as the bullwhip. Without that snap of the whip there is no power, no force, no true strength. The snap is the FOCUS of the blow. Without timing every muscle of your body to tense simultaneously at the point of impact, there will be no real power, no real strength, no real force.

Striking

Complete relaxation — Tension (Coil) Thrust — Impact — Focus (Complete Tension) — Complete Relaxation (No residual tension should remain.)

Soft — Hard — Soft

11. Force and Direction

One must apply force directly through the opponent's center of gravity if he is to be moved in the direction of the force, otherwise the force rolls off him and he rolls off the force.

12. Force and the Base Of Support

Whenever punching or kicking keep the supporting base, the soles of the feet, flat. Then the law of reaction will be obeyed.

13. The Power Of Circularity

The wheel and axle are examples of devices that illustrate perfectly the power of using circular strikes and parries. The wheel and the axle device consists of a wheel attached to a central axle about which it revolves. Force may be applied to the wheel either at the rim as in the case of the steering wheel of the automobile or to the axle, as in the case of the automobile's rear wheels.

The application of circular force in defending oneself is based upon applying force to the wheel at the rim. The attacker's body is the axle, his arm is the spoke, his wrist is the rim of the wheel. The defender, by grabbing, locking or pulling, can apply force on the attacker's wrist and unbalance or throw him.

The application of circular force in attacking is based upon applying force to the axle. Using the power of his hips and legs the attacker revolves his body as an axle and transfers this generated power through his arms to his fists or through his legs to his feet to focus on his opponent.

The steering wheel is an example of a wheel and axle which magnifies force at the expense of speed and distance. The longer the diameter of the wheel, the greater the magnification of force. The large circle sacrifices speed and distance for more force. The small circle sacrifices force for speed and distance.

C. THE NAMES AND THE ORDER
OF THE EIGHTY-EIGHT FORMS

1. Step Forward and (Right) Punch
2. (Right) Raise Hands and Step Back
3. Step Forward, (Left) Deflect Up and (Right) Punch
4. (Left) Lower Parry and (Right) Punch
5. Change Steps, Step Forward and Apply Left Shoulder
6. Hit Tiger Right (Raise Step Return)
7. Strike with Left Elbow
8. Push with Right Hand
9. Strike Opponent with Left Backfist
10. Sidestep, Step Forward and Apply Right Shoulder
11. Hit Tiger Left (Raise Step Return)
12. Sidestep, Strike Opponent with Right Backfist
13. (Right) Raise Hands and Step Forward (Change Steps)
14. Turn Right and Push
15. "Fold and Pile" Applying Right Backfist
16. (Left) Deflect Up and (Right) Punch
17. Diagonal (Right) Forearm Strike
18. Parting of Wild Horse's Mane — Left (Change Steps)
19. Hit Tiger Right (Below) (Raise Step Return)
20. Turn Left, Step Back, Pull Back
21. Step Up and Apply Left Shoulder
22. Push Against Left Wrist and Elbow (Change Steps)
23. Retreat To Ride The Tiger — Left Style (Below — Right Foot Kicks Up)
24. (Right) Punch Opponent's Pubic Region (Change Steps)
25. (Right) Wrist-pull, (Right) Forearm Smash (Recoil Step)
26. Fair Lady Works At Shuttles, Right (Change Steps)
27. (Left) Deflect Up and (Right) Punch (Return Step)
28. White Crane Extends Its Wings (Below — Left Foot Kicks Up)
29. Step Forward and Apply Left Shoulder
30. (Left) Step Back, Raise Step Return (Right) and Apply Left Arm-twist
31. Turn Left, Pull Back and Push
32. Double Wind Blows Against Ears

33. Two Hands Push (Change Steps)
34. (Left) Move Aside and (Right) Punch
35. Single (Left) Hand Push Against Right Arm
36. Apply Snapping Armlock
37. Follow Through with (Left Hand) Push
38. Neutralize and Strike with Right Palm
39. Neutralize and (Left) Push (Change Steps)
40. Neutralize and Strike with Right Elbow
41. (Right) Elbow-pull and (Right) Forearm Smash (Change Steps)
42. (Right) Arm-twist (Change Steps)
43. Hit Tiger Right (Raise Step Return)
44. Turn Left, Step Back, Pull Back
45. Step Forward and Apply Left Shoulder
46. Raise Step Return and Press Forward
47. Separate Arms and Apply Right Shoulder (Change Steps)
48. Apply Left Shoulder (Change Steps)
49. Strike with Right Elbow
50. Turn Left, Step Up, Golden Cock Stands On One Leg — Right
51. Retreat Pulling Down On Opponent's Wrists
52. Kick with Left Sole
53. Turn, Step Up and Apply Left Shoulder
54. Step Back and Strike with Right Arm
55. Turn Left (Change Steps) and Separate Right Foot
56. (Left) Deflect Up and Brush Knee Right
57. Turn Right (Change Steps) and Separate Left Foot
58. (Right) Deflect Up and Brush Knee Left
59. Change Hands and Apply Right Shoulder (Change Steps)
60. Sidestep, Return Right Shoulder Strike (Return Step)
61. Grasp Bird's Tail Left (Change Steps)
62. Wave Hands Like Clouds — Right
63. Grasp Bird's Tail Right (Change Steps)
64. Wave Hands Like Clouds — Left
65. Open Arms and Strike with Right Backhand (Push Up Form)
66. Right Backfist Parry and (Right) Uppercutting Punch (Raise Step Return)
67. High Pat On Horse (Above — Left Palm Thrust) (Below — Left Foot Kicks Up) (Change Steps)
68. White Crane Extends Its Wings — Left Style (Above — Right Palm Thrust) (Below — Right Foot Kicks Up)
69. Turn Around and Position the Lotus (Change Steps)
70. Slanting Flying Left (Change Steps)

71. Step Back, Snake Creeps Down, Knife Hand Thrust
72. Slanting Flying Right (Change Steps)
73. Hit Tiger Left (Raise Step Return)
74. Sidestep, Strike Opponent with Right Backfist
75. Fall Back and Twist Like Monkey — Left
76. Step Up and Thrust Out with Left Palm
77. Fall Back and Twist Like Monkey — Right
78. Right Palm (Reverse) Thrust
79. Fall Back and Twist Like Monkey — Left (Follow Through with a Quick Forward Shift and a Right Palm Reverse Thrust)
80. Step Up and Form Seven Stars (Below — Right Foot Kicks Up)
81. Sea Bottom Needle
82. Fan Through The Back (Change Steps)
83. Play Guitar
84. Shoot Tiger with Drawn Bow
85. Turn and Execute Single Whip (Change Steps) (Right Dragon-head Backwrist Strike)
86. Elbow Under Fist (Change Steps)
87. Cross Hands (Change Steps)
88. Carry Tiger Home to the Mountains

■

chapter VII

VII. TAI CHI WEAPONS

A. INTRODUCTION
B. TAI CHI SWORD
   1. Song
   2. The Names and the Order of the Fifty-Four Forms
C. TAI CHI BROADSWORD (KNIFE)
   1. Song
   2. The Names and the Order of the Thirty-Two Forms

VII. TAI CHI WEAPONS

A. INTRODUCTION

Weapons are merely an extension of the human body. The application of weapons is therefore based upon one's proficiency in empty hand forms and movements. One must therefore master Tai Chi's 82 before one is permitted to learn the movements of the Tai Chi weapons.

Although there are such Tai Chi weapons as the quarter staff and bullwhip, only the sword and broadsword will be discussed. One major clarification will be made with the terms sword and broadsword. In Chinese a sword is any blade with two cutting or sharp edges and a knife is any blade with one cutting or sharp edge. So as not to confuse Westerners, I used the designation Tai Chi broadsword to point out that the weapon is not a knife as the Chinese would call it.

In terms of footwork the Tai Chi broadsword is more intricate than the Tai Chi sword movements. In terms of the fine techniques of striking and blocking the Tai Chi sword is more intricate, fine and complex. Weapon training in Tai Chi in this day and age serves mainly as a method to self-awareness and as a method to strengthen the upper limbs and torso. Holding and swinging a heavy weapon slowly builds up the muscles of the hand, arms and upper torso. The general principles and rules of the Soft Fist apply throughout the weapon training as they also do in empty hand training.

B. TAI CHI SWORD

1.   SONG

   From the very beginning, the Art of the Sword was not easy
   to transmit. Like the dragon. Like the rainbow the Art
   of the Sword was very mysterious and profound.
   If you cut and chop using the Sword like a knife, then old
   Master Chang will laugh to death at you.

2.   THE NAMES AND THE ORDER OF THE FIFTY-FOUR FORMS

   (1) The Rise of the Tai Chi Sword

(2) Step Up and Enclose with Sword
(3) Immortal Fairy Points the Way
(4) Three Rings Envelop the Moon
(5) Big Top Star
(6) Swallow Brushes the Water
(7) Left and Right — Parry and Sweep
(8) Little Top Star
(9) Honey Bee Enters the Honeycomb
(10) Clever Cat Catches a Rat
(11) Dragon Fly Touches the Water
(12) Swallow Enters the Nest
(13) Phoenix Extends Both Wings
(14) Right Turning Wind (Blows A Figure Eight)
(15) Little Top Star
(16) Left Spinning Wind (Blows A Figure Eight)
(17) Waiting for the Fish
(18) Brush Aside the Grass and Look for the Snake
(19) Embrace the Moon to Bosom
(20) Send the Bird Up the Tree
(21) Black Dragon Swings Its Tail
(22) Wind Swirls the Lotus Leaves
(23) Lion Waves Its Head
(24) Tiger Embraces His Head
(25) Wild Horse Leaps Over the Stream
(26) Turn Over and Rein In the Horse
(27) Needle Points South (Chinese Compass)
(28) Welcoming Wind Flicks Dust
(29) Follow the Water and Push the Boat
(30) Shooting Star Follows the Moon
(31) Sky Bird Flys Over the Waterfall
(32) Lift Up the Curtains
(33) Left and Right — Wheeling Sword
(34) Swallow Mouths the Earth
(35) Great Condor Spreads Its Wings
(36) Moon Forages the Sea Bottom
(37) Embrace the Moon to Bosom
(38) Night Demon Explores the Sea
(39) Rhinoceros Watches the Moon
(40) Shoot the Geese
(41) Green Dragon Explores with Its Claws
(42) Phoenix Extends Both Wings

(43) Left and Right — Ride and Counter
(44) Shoot the Geese
(45) White Monkey Presents Fruit
(46) Falling Flowers
(47) Fair Lady Works at Shuttles
(48) White Tiger Plays with Its Tail
(49) Fish Jumped Over the Dragon Door
(50) Black Dragon Twists Around a Column
(51) Immortal Fairy Points the Way
(52) Wind Sweeps the Plum Blossoms
(53) Hands Present the Ivory Scroll
(54) Sword Returns to Its Embracing Origin

C. TAI CHI BROADSWORD (KNIFE)

1.   SONG

With Show and Pride, The Seven Stars Ride The Tiger.
(Movement 1 — 3)

White Crane Extends Its Wings Hiding Its Legs Below.
(Movement 4)

With Its Leaves Hidden Below, The Lotus Flowers Sway to The Wind.
(Movement 5)

Push Open The Window And Watch The Long Crescent-Shaped Moon.
(Movement 6)

Look To The Left. Look To The Right. Two Parts Divide.
(Movement 7 — 9)

When Fair Lady Works At Shuttles, She Reacts To The Eight Directions.
(Movement 10)

With A Ball Before Him, The Lion Rolls, Circles And Plays With It.
(Movement 11 — 12d)

The Mountain Opens. A Super-Giant Snake Turns Around And Slithers Off.
(Movement 12e — 13)

Left, Right, High, Low, The Butterfly Wings Lovingly Around The Flowers.
(Movement 14 — 16)

Turn Around, Thrust And Parry Like A Weather Vane.
(Movement 17 — 20)

Raising Both Legs Precede Hit Tiger Form.
(Movement 21 — 22)

Legs Coordinated And Synchronized Strike Out At Half Body Slant.
(Movement 23 — 24)

Follow The Water And Push The Boat. Then Knife Is Flipped Over And Brought Down Like A Whip And Then Used Like A Pole.
(Movement 25 — 27)

Turn Over, Divide Your Hands and Leap Over The Dragon Door.
(Movement 28)

With All Your Strength Split Open Wah Mountain And Then Execute Carry Knife Form.
(Movement 29 — 30)

LOOK WALL Carries Stone. Phoenix Returns To Its Nest.
(Movement 31 — 32)

2. THE NAMES AND THE ORDER OF THE THIRTY-TWO FORMS

(1) The Opening of the Tai Chi Knife
(2) Step Up and Form Seven Stars (Left Style) (Kicking Form)
(3) Turn Left, Step Up and Form Seven Stars (Right Style) (Kicking Form)
(4) White Crane Extends Its Wings (Retreat To Ride The Tiger)
(5) Spiral Around Low and Hide Level Knife
(6) Pushing Slanting—Vertical Knife
(7) Teasing Knife Left
(8) Teasing Circular Knife Right
    a. Teasing Knife Left
    b. Teasing Circular Knife Right
    c. Teasing Knife Left

  (9) Confronting Push Knife

(10) Fair Lady Works at Shuttles

           (Turn Around, Circle and Swing Knife Counterclockwise Overhead; Embrace Knife; Night Demon Points Out the Way; Brush Aside the Grass and Sweep the Legs)

(11) Level Pull

(12) Push Diagonal—Level Knife

      a.   Level Pull

      b.   Push Diagonal—Level Knife

      c.   Level Pull

      d.   Push Diagonal—Level Knife

      e.   Confronting Push Knife

      f.   Turn and Hide Knife

(13) Circle and Swing Knife Clockwise Around Head and Hide Knife

(14) Shaving Up to the Left

(15) Striking Down to the Right

      a.   Shaving Up to the Left

      b.   Striking Down to the Right

(16) Confronting Push Knife

(17) Turn Around and Hide Knife

      a.   Swing Vertical—Clockwise Circling Knife and Hide Knife

(18) Upper Cutting Knife

(19) Smashing Ferris-Wheel Knife

(20) Upper Cutting Knife

(21) Raising Legs: One and Two

(22) Step Back and Hit Tiger Right

      a.   Hide Knife

      b.   Circle and Swing Knife Clockwise Around Head and Hide Knife

(23) Legs Coordinated, Synchronized and Applied Like the Loving Inseparability of Male—Female

(24) Turn Completely (360 Degrees) Around, Circle and Swing Counterclockwise Knife Around Head, and Hide Knife

(25) Follow the Water and Push the Boat

      a.   Turn Around and Whip Knife

      b.   Whip Knife Becomes Pole

      c.   Turn Around and Hide Knife

■

chapter VIII ⎯⎯⎯⎯⎯⎯⎯⎯

VIII. THE MASTER—PUPIL RELATIONSHIP

It is of the utmost importance for one to understand the relationship between master and pupil. Unless one does, one can never be free to discover the riches that lie beyond the scope of the mind. For the mind that makes this discovery, there is joy.

Most of the relationships between master and pupil are relationships of power. Power always centralizes. Power always corrupts.

The one who knows has power over the one who does not know simply because the one who does not know desires to have what the one who knows has. The pupil who does not know learns from the master through his obedience, self-sacrifice, recognition and acceptance of his master's authority.

When one learns from a famous master, one also gives oneself importance. One says that he is a member of such and such an organization led by so and so. The master says he has thousands of pupils in his organization in every part of the world. Thus, through recognition, the master and pupil gain status.

The pressures of life have become too great. One is now lonely, fearful and confused. One wants to be free from this state of conflict and to be comforted. The master is one who is supposed to have experienced the state of no conflict, and therefore he is an authority on it. So one attaches oneself to the master and accepts his authority in the belief that he can lead one out of his state of confusion to the state of satori.

One doesn't realize that to be led and to be guided is to become a slave. If one is a slave, how can one ever know freedom? One must first be free to experience enlightenment. But the master who knows is already a slave to his own knowledge and experience. The experience is of knowledge from the past.

One doesn't try to solve one's own problems because one is just plain lazy. It is easier to have someone take over and tell one what to do.

Life is movement from moment to moment. Finding is from moment to moment. Freedom lies in movement of moment to moment discovery. Enlightenment can be only in a state of freedom. Therefore, how can the master guide or lead us to that which is forever constantly in movement?

It is ridiculous to deceive oneself by thinking that one really seeks enlightenment by joining an organization or practicing a method. One will find that enlightenment is not the factor that keeps one loyal to the master and his organization. It is the comfort and security that it can give to one's life that does. The master and his organization cannot lead one out of his state of conflict. It is understanding that makes it possible for one to see the truth. Truth liberates.

The master asserts that he knows, that through his technique and his methods one can *experience* enlightenment, that one can be led stage by stage and level by level, graduating from the bottom to the top. So the whole system of different levels of position and authority and of prestige and status is created. How can all these divisions between master and pupil lead to Communion? Without Communion how can there be enlightenment?

In teaching a method, the master only further conditions one's mind. How can a conditioned mind be free? All methods are developed on a pattern. The pattern creates the system. The system may give its results and rewards, but life is not a result or a reward. It just is.

The followers as well as the masters are products of the system they created. If the system leads them to enlightenment, then the system, not enlightenment, would be the dominating factor. If the system is the dominating factor, there can be no freedom. Freedom must be in the beginning or liberation cannot be. Freedom is beyond all systems.

Clarity cannot be given by another, even if he is called a master. For example, I always say to all my new students that I am not a master, that I have essentially nothing to teach, and that I am as much a pupil as they are a master. Intelligence cannot be legislated.

Enlightenment will come not through method or invitation. It will come subtly and softly when the self is not, when thought is not, when the mind is not. In that state one will know what it is to be free, to discover and to love. Love admits no division. The relationship between master and pupil is one of division. Through that relationship Love is denied. Love is and will do what it will.

■

chapter IX

IX. TAI CHI CHUAN: EXPERIENCES AND LESSONS

A. EXPERIENCES
1. Experience One
2. Experience Two: During the Practice of Tai Chi's Eighty-Eight
3. Experience Three: During the Practice of Joined Hands
4. Experience Four: During the Practice of Tai Chi's Eighty-Two

B. LESSONS
1. Characteristics of Experiences
2. Reaction Following Experiences
3. Significance of Experiences
4. The Significance of the Grand Ultimate

IX. TAI CHI CHUAN: EXPERIENCES AND LESSONS

A. EXPERIENCES

1. EXPERIENCE ONE

I was in the midst of it all. There was no doubt. Fatigue was setting in. I was becoming very tired. Conflict surrounded me. The vroom, vroom, vroom of the big guns going off thundered in my ears. Tracers like falling stars littered the sky. The rat-tat-tat of the machine guns and the spray of bullets forced me deeper into my foxhole. The jets whined overhead and the flash of the rockets and the flaming napalm lit the sky and landscape like a million neon signs on Broadway. The stench of burned, dead and dying flesh was overwhelming. A flood of tears washed my eyes of the sting of the heavy, black, burnt-powder smoke. It was midnight, and the battle had raged all day. The ache of tired flesh was slowly overcoming me. I tried but I couldn't stay awake any longer. Finally I faded away from the noise and died into the night.

Is it odd that the mind is like an endless battleground? It is forever chattering and thinking. It is full of drive, effort and activity. No matter how hard we try, the effort just makes the mind more restless than ever.

When I woke, it was day. A strange feeling had settled over me. I could see on this clear, blue morning the burned out shells of machines and men littered everywhere. In the midst of the battle it was difficult and impossible to know what was really going on. Now the guns had stopped and the battle was over. One could survey the terrain and see all that had taken place.

No one knew how or when the battle would end or what it would be like after it had. The mind was like that. For no apparent reason the madness all ended. The chattering stopped. In the moment I just was. I could see the whole of life crystal clear around me. As I walked among the people I could see the truth of life etched out on their faces. There was much sadness and sorrow. In looking out, I was looking in. Yet there was a joy in me that was inexplicable. That joy was inexhaustible. Whatever I did appeared completely effortless. I was floating across the land. I lost all sense of time. I found that the world was me and that I was the world. I found that in the expenditure of energy, there was also the gathering of energy. There was perfect discipline and spontaneity acting simultaneously. For no apparent reason the feeling left me as subtly as it had come. All that was left was a memory of a peace that had no depth, a silence that was totally overwhelming and a serenity that was so profound and mystifying as to be beyond human imagination.

Endless battle and conflict destroy the mind's sensitivity. Only peace can bring harmony and balance. The mind is in that state when one is in the state of experiencing Tai Chi, the Grand Ultimate. The experiencing of the Grand Ultimate is necessary for the renewal of the mind. Without renewal the mind is forever in the past.

2. EXPERIENCE TWO: DURING THE PRACTICE OF TAI CHI'S EIGHTY-EIGHT

I was the center and yet I was not. The center was everywhere and yet I was in perfect balance. I was giving my full attention to my partner, to his punches and his kicks and yet I could see myself at the same time looking on from outside like a spectator watching a boxing match. I was doing and yet it seemed I was not, for everything was totally effortless. I know it took time to go through that pattern and yet there was no sense of time. There was no discipline, no force, no effort and yet everything was done with perfect technique and power. There was much physical movement and great mental attention and yet there was no lack of energy. Despite the paradox, the contradiction, my mind and my body coordinated perfectly. The balance and harmony could be felt in the pervading sense of silence and peace.

The mind, ruminating on the whole experience, saw it as a paradox. During the experience the mind was aware of the paradox. This demonstrates that the doing of anything is always now, producing the reality of feelings and emotions. Thinking about the past is done in the present. Thinking about the future is also done in the present. Thinking is the paradox and the contradiction. The feeling and doing now is never paradoxical, it just occurs.

3. EXPERIENCE THREE: DURING THE PRACTICE OF JOINED HANDS

I never thought it was possible. But here I was, doing it. I was actually able to stick and not resist while my opponent was coming full blast with his arm firing out and then withdrawing instantly. We were going full tilt and at full speed. The flow was unbelievably fast. Like all the other experiences all was effortless, all was timeless, all was peaceful.

4. EXPERIENCE FOUR: DURING THE PRACTICE OF TAI CHI'S EIGHTY-TWO

I could see everything with crystal clarity. I was loose and relaxed. I was the flow. There was not I on one hand, the flow on the other. The movement was effortless. There was no sense of time, of effort, of doing or of controlling. I was flying. The peace was absolutely overpowering. When the experience ended, I cried. I never desired such silence and such serenity so much. I knew then that to die in that state is to know how to live.

B. LESSONS

1. CHARACTERISTICS OF EXPERIENCES

These experiences have certain common characteristics. First, one does not enter the state with a bang. One's movement into it is so subtle that one is there before one knows it. Second, there is the paradox of one being there and not being there, of being out there looking in at oneself. Third, there is the sense of being stable and fixed in one place and yet being positioned everywhere simultaneously. Fourth, there is the feeling of doing and not doing, of everything being done with no effort. Fifth, there is the sense of moving and yet not moving as if one is totally still. Sixth, there is the feeling of no time. Seventh, there is the sense that no matter how much one has done, no energy has been spent, but that energy has been gathered instead. Eighth, there is the sense that no one was in control and yet everything was done perfectly. Ninth, there is the absolutely overpowering and overwhelming feeling of peace, silence and serenity, a feeling that is indescribable.

2. REACTION FOLLOWING EXPERIENCES

The first reaction after such an experience is one of awe. Then one tries to recall the whole experience detail by detail. Finally one tries to regain and relive the experience by repeating and imitating what one had done before. One will learn that one cannot recreate such an experience by any method. One can create a similar experience, but the mind, as the self, as the I, as the Ego, is always aware of all that is happening and is at the same time in control of the situation. It is very much like a drug-induced experience in which one can be aware of what is happening to oneself. The real experience is never under any control. The I, the Ego, the Self are in a state of total paradox in the real experience.

All the experiences might have common characteristics, but they are nevertheless all different and yet they are all the same. The experiences in themselves and in relation to other similar experiences seem always the same and yet paradoxically different. These experiences cannot be brought about; they come at the most unexpected times and places. They will come when one is not, and they go when one reflects.

3. SIGNIFICANCE OF EXPERIENCES

These experiences teach us several significant things. One learns that one can never know the truth of anything without first-hand or direct experience; that doing is always more important than seeking a result; that understanding is more important than accumulating knowledge; that understanding the attitudes of one human being to another is the understanding of the relationship of an individual to society. One learns that there is a bliss that pervades the whole of human life through the silence of Tai Chi and the peace of the Grand Ultimate.

(1) FIRST-HAND EXPERIENCE

The majority of us are accustomed to approaching each other through an image. The advertising agencies have conditioned us to accept images and symbols as a way of life and to make these images almost into reality. Always meet another openly and directly, not as a collision of images.

(2) THE ATTITUDE AND APPROACH OF ONE HUMAN BEING TO ANOTHER

When one plays a game with others, everyone must accept the rules of the game or not play. To accept these rules is to accept the approach to others in good faith. The point of the game is not to win or to lose. The spirit of the game is to do. The beauty of life lies in the joy of being together and doing together, not gaining some end.

(3) HUMAN RELATIONSHIP

If one has a job and the work is very demanding, it is no problem as long as the people one works with are in harmony. The people will help and the workload will be spread out. If the people are not cooperative, it doesn't matter if the workload is light or heavy, the situation will become intolerable and one either quits his job or becomes extremely unhappy.

4. THE SIGNIFICANCE OF THE GRAND ULTIMATE

Through the practice of Chuan one may or may not experience Tai Chi, the Grand Ultimate. These experiences that I have spoken of are experiences of Tai Chi, the Grand Ultimate. To have such experience is to communicate with one's beginning while one is living. To do so is to tap that inexhaustible source of all life.

The source of all life is boundless and limitless. To tap the source is to tap the common bond that ties man to man and man to all living things. To tap the source is also to know the meaning of Communion which is the ability to meet another person on the same level at the same time. Communion is Integration. Integration leads to Harmony. Harmony is Love. Love is Totality. Totality is Tai Chi. Tai Chi is the Grand Ultimate. The Grand Ultimate is the Source, the Beginning, the Cause of all Causes.

It may be true that no means, no path can lead to the infinite, to Tai Chi, the Grand Ultimate. Yet one can experience and commune with it. The Grand Ultimate can come to you. When it does, it does so of its own accord. Finite consciousness can never touch or know it. When finite consciousness is not present, then the mind is open, vulnerable and receptive. Only the perceptive, responsive mind has the possibility of communing with the Ineffable.

Always remember that my descriptions are not the thing itself. The thing itself in the final analysis cannot be given by one to another. Because it is fundamentally ineffable, no word, no symbol can contain it. The infinite contains all that is finite.

■

chapter X

X. THE GRADING SYSTEM OF THE YANG SCHOOL OF TAI CHI CHUAN

A. THE NINE LEVELS: TAI CHI CREST
B. CURRICULUM

X. THE GRADING SYSTEM
OF
THE YANG SCHOOL OF TAI CHI CHUAN

A. THE NINE LEVELS: TAI CHI CREST

The Tai Chi Crest with the corresponding colors designates the levels of competence from a beginner's level one up to an advanced level nine. Black and White Crest of the beginner and the advanced student on level nine is consistent with the basic philosophy of the Soft Fist. Knowledge has levels but learning has none. Learning is an on-going process.

This grading system for Tai Chi Chuan is a personal creation of mine. Under the old system that I studied, students were designated as junior, intermediate or senior. Under the old system, junior students would be equivalent to my first level of Black and White. Intermediate students would be equivalent to my second and third level of Black and Red, and Black and Orange. Senior students would be considered anyone at level four, Black and Yellow Crest or higher.

1. Black and White
2. Black and Red
3. Black and Orange
4. Black and Yellow
5. Black and Green
6. Black and Blue
7. Black and Purple
8. Black and Brown
9. Black and White

B. CURRICULUM

1. Black and White
    (1) Basic Principles and Techniques of Breathing
    (2) Tai Chi's 82 — Right Style
    (3) Eight Fundamental Forms of Joined Hands
2. Black and Red
    (1) Integration of Eight Simple Forms
    (2) Standing Four Hands
    (3) Walking Four Hands

3. Black and Orange
   (1) Integration of Eight Simple Forms with the Standing Four Hands
   (2) Integration of Eight Simple Forms with Walking Joined Hands
   (3) Changing Steps from Corresponding to Opposite Steps to Corresponding Steps
   (4) Walking Four Hands and Tight Circle
4. Black and Yellow
   (1) Tai Chi's 82 — Left Style
   (2) Ta Lu
      (a) Fixed
      (b) Random
   (3) Walking Four Hands and Ta Lu and Walking Four Hands
5. Black and Green
   (1) Tai Chi's 88 — Applications: Right and Left
   (2) Mixture within Tai Chi's 88
6. Black and Blue
   (1) Integration of Walking Four Hands — Ta Lu — Application
7. Black and Purple
   (1) Sword
8. Black and Brown
   (1) Broadsword
   (2) Broadsword vs. Broadsword
9. Black and White
   (1) Philosophy and History of the Soft Fist and the Yang School of Tai Chi Chuan
   (2) Tai Chi's 82 in a Four-Foot Circle
   (3) Other Forms of Tai Chi Chuan
   (4) Tai Chi's 24 — The Short Yang
   (5) Self-Defense Techniques from Other Soft Fist Schools

■

bibliography ───────────────────

HISTORY

Chen, Yim Lum. *Tai Chi Chuan: Knife, Sword, Staff, Free Sparring, Compiled*. Hong Kong. (Chinese Edition Only).

Draeger, Donn F. and Robert W. Smith. *Asian Fighting Arts*. Kodansha International Ltd. Tokyo and Palo Alto. 1969.

Maisel, Edward. *Tai Chi For Health*. Prentice-Hall, Inc. Englewood Cliffs, New Jersey. 1963.

PHILOSOPHY

Fromm, Erich. *The Art Of Loving*. Harper and Row, Publishers, Inc. 1967.

Krishnamurti, J. *Commentaries On Living. Series 1, 2 and 3*. Quest Books. Theosophical Publishing House. Wheaton, Illinois. 1968.

Watts, Alan W. *The Way of Zen*. Vintage Books. A Division of Random House. New York. 1957.
The Meaning Of Happiness. Perennial Library. Harper and Row, Publisher. New York. 1968.

Welch, Holmes. *Taoism: The Parting Of The Way*. Saunders of Toronto, Ltd. 1967.

■